O.D.W.A.B.D.A.N.O.T.W.M

One Day
We'll All
Be Dead

SCAACHI KOUL

and None
of This
Will Matter

Picador | New York

ONE DAY WE'LL ALL BE DEAD AND NONE OF THIS WILL MATTER. Copyright © 2017 by Scaachi Koul. All rights reserved. Printed in the United States of America. For information, address Picador, 175 Fifth Avenue, New York, N.Y. 10010.

picadorusa.com • picadorbookroom.tumblr.com
twitter.com/picadorusa • facebook.com/picadorusa

Picador® is a U.S. registered trademark and is used by Macmillan Publishing Group, LLC, under license from Pan Books Limited.

For book club information, please visit facebook.com/picadorbookclub or e-mail marketing@picadorusa.com.

Portions of the following essays were previously published in different form: "Inheritance Tax" in *Hazlitt*; "A Good Egg" in *Hazlitt*; "Hunting Season" in *Buzzfeed*; "Tawi River, Elbow River" in *Buzzfeed*; and "Size Me Up" in *The Walrus*.

Designed by CS Richardson

The Library of Congress Cataloging-in-Publication Data is available upon request.

ISBN 978-1-250-12102-8 (trade paperback)
ISBN 978-1-250-12107-3 (e-book)

Our books may be purchased in bulk for promotional, educational, or business use. Please contact your local bookseller or the Macmillan Corporate and Premium Sales Department at 1-800-221-7945, extension 5442, or by e-mail at Macmillan SpecialMarkets@macmillan.com.

First published by Doubleday, a division of Penguin Random House Canada.

First U.S. Edition: May 2017

10 9 8 7 6 5 4 3

FOR MY PARENTS, WHO WILL OUTLIVE US ALL,
ONE WAY OR ANOTHER.

O.D.W.A.B.D.A.N.O.T.W.M

Inheritance Tax

———

O nly idiots aren't afraid of flying. Planes are inherently unnatural; your body isn't supposed to be launched into the sky, and few people comprehend the science that keeps them from tumbling into the ocean. Do you know how many planes crash every year? Neither do I, but I know the answer is more than one, WHICH IS ENOUGH.

My boyfriend finds my fear of flying hilarious at best and deeply frustrating at worst. For my twenty-fourth birthday, he booked us a trip to Southeast Asia for two weeks, the farthest I've been from home in more than a decade. Plenty of people take a gap year between high school and university to travel, or spend a summer back-packing through Europe to "find" themselves. (A bullshit statement if ever there was one. Where do you think you'll be? No one finds anything in France except bread and pretension, and frankly, both of those are in my lap *right now*.) I never did this. I talked about wanting to, sure, listing all the places I would go one day, hoping to have my photo taken next to a crumbling edifice in Brazil or with a charming street merchant in Laos. When I was thirteen, my mom asked me where I'd get the money to travel and I said, "From you, of course." She laughed me straight out of her kitchen nook. Travelling tells the world that you're educated, that you're willing to take risks, that you have earned your condescension. But do you know what my apartment has that no other place does? All my stuff. All the things that let me dull out the reminders of my human existence, that let me forget that the world is full of dark, impenetrable crags. I have, I think, a healthy fear of dying, and marching forward into the uncharted is almost asking for it. But it was my birthday, and my beautiful idiot boyfriend was offering to take me some-place exciting. He suggested Thailand and Vietnam, because he likes the sun and I like peanut sauces. I agreed, my haunches already breaking out in a very familiar rash.

As we made our way from Toronto to Chicago, then Chicago to Tokyo, then Tokyo to Bangkok, he was a paragon of serenity. (He's older than me by more than a decade, and acts it whenever we do something new, largely because, comparatively, almost everything is new to me and nothing is new to him.) He was a latchkey kid, permitted to wander his small town in the '80s and '90s in a way that feels nostalgic to him and like the beginning of a documentary about child abduction to me. He smoked and drank and cried and laughed and was freer at twelve than I have ever been. While our plane started to taxi, I squeezed his meaty forearm as if I was tenderizing a ham hock – rubbing his white skin red and twisting his blond arm hair into little knots – and he just gazed dreamily out the window. When we took off, my throat started to close and I wanted to be home, stay home, never leave home.

I wasn't raised with a fear of flying. My parents were afraid of plenty of things that would likely never affect us – murderers lurking in our backyard, listeria in our sandwich meat, *vegans* – but dying on a plane was all too mundane for them. We used to take plenty of trips together and separately, and lengthy air travel played an unavoidable role in their origin story. They emigrated from India in the late 1970s and flew back for visits every few years. For vacations or my dad's business trips, they flew to St. Thomas and Greece and Montreal and New York. Mom didn't like bugs and Papa didn't like small dogs, but I don't remember either of them being particularly fearful.

I wasn't always afraid of flying either. When I travelled with my parents as a kid, air travel was exciting. I got to

buy new notebooks and travel games, and flight attendants packed cookies and chips and mini cans of ginger
ale in airsickness bags and handed them out to the kids
mid-flight. 9/11 hadn't happened, so our family wasn't
yet deemed suspicious at Calgary's airport. I once loudly
asked my brother while standing in a security queue
how, exactly, people made bombs out of batteries while
waving around a pack of thirty AAs intended for a video
game. My parents let me eat a whole Toblerone bar and
then I threw up in a translucent gift bag while we waited
in line to board. I was alive!

Flying became a necessity by the time I was seventeen,
the only way to stay connected with my family rather
than a conduit for mile-high vomiting. When I graduated
from high school, instead of doing what so many of my
classmates did – a month in Italy here, three months in
Austria there – I moved across the country almost immediately to start university. If I wanted to see my parents (and
I did, as my homesickness burst wide open the second my
parents dropped me off at my residence), I would have to
fly. Three, sometimes four times a year, I'd take a four-
hour flight to see people who I knew were at least legally
obligated to love me.

But by my early twenties, years into this routine, something shifted and made room for fear to set in. Turbulence
wasn't fun anymore; it didn't feel like a ride, it felt like the
beginning of my early death. I'd start crying during take-
off, sure that the plane would plummet. Flight attendants

about her first impression upon actually seeing my dad, she merely pursed her lips and continued folding towels, saying, "I thought he was okay." This, the great love affair that spawned me, a woman who would one day get both of her hands stuck in two different salsa jars at the same time.

My dad asked her father for her hand (and the rest of her, presumably) when she was just eighteen, about to head off to university away from their small town in Kashmir. My grandfather said no, but to try again when she was older. He was a police sergeant, but a gentle guy who rarely raised his voice or grew upset. My mom did not inherit his calmness – he yelled at her once when she was twelve and she felt so wronged that she launched a hunger strike, one that lasted entire *hours*. He apologized by placing his hat at her feet, begging her to please just eat something. (I did the same at eleven, but my parents just shrugged and said there were bagels in the fridge when I was ready – brown people don't know what to do with bread.) When Mom was twenty-two, my dad was approved, and they were engaged and married within a year. Another year and some later, they had my brother. Soon after that, my dad moved to Southern Ontario; his family waited months before joining him.

But before this, there was the big death that marked Papa just after the birth of his first child in India. My brother was small enough to sleep between his paternal grandparents on the flat roof of their home during a mercilessly hot night. My grandmother, in her fifties at the time, woke up and took him inside to change his diaper. When she returned, her husband didn't wake up: he had died of a massive heart attack in his sleep. Mom says they found him with his hand on his heart. My dad was only thirty. He doesn't talk about it. We don't ask.

My father's mother, Behenji, lived with us in Calgary when I was young but she hated the cold and didn't speak any English and I didn't understand who or what she was. She opted to leave after a few years, something that infuriated Papa because wasn't it his job, as the eldest son, to take care of her? It didn't matter that she was generally in good health or always prickly or maintained her usual routines, he feared for her constantly. Near the end, she started to get confused and would forget things or people or where she was. Papa would sit in his armchair, clenching his teeth, ruminating on how he'd abandoned her years before. "I've asked her to stay put until I come, but who knows," Papa said to me, two years before she died, as if he could tell her body not to retreat. "If she has to go, I hope she goes in my arms. That will be the culmination of a life. Of a life well lived. A hard life. She had a hard life." He was on the phone with me at the time, speaking to me mostly in sighs and rueful grunts, a language I've since learned to speak myself.

Behenji lived into her eighties, thirty-odd years after her husband had passed, dying when my dad was already in his mid-sixties. Now, he does long-distance running daily and takes multivitamins the size of horse tranquilizers every morning. He has high blood pressure and high out of a lamb bone with shocking fervour, then stuck her tongue through the hollow to tease me about how truly, deeply gross I found it. Mom made rotis from scratch, kneading the atta with her hands and then dragging a knife across her skin to gather the excess, laughing at seven-year-old me recoiling in horror. Mom's arthritis got worse but she kept cooking rogan josh so spicy it ripped the roof of your mouth clean off, whipping a wooden spoon around a pressure cooker with her aching wrist. Mom yelled. Mom told you how she felt, when she felt it, as much and as often as she needed to tell you. Mom cried all the time, happy or sad, her tears running a moat around a mole just under her eye, her face like a Shiva Lingam for feelings. And Mom was not afraid of you. When Papa was angry, or afraid, or nervous, or happy, or thrilled, he just seethed quietly because it was all too much to handle. Mom, on the other hand, hugged you with her arms and shoulders and suffocating bosom, burying you in all her soft, cool flesh. That, or she would kill you. These were your options.

And yet even when my mom was at her bravest, I was gearing up for death. I invented diseases for myself and was sure they'd kill me. By the time I was seven, I started running my fingers up and down my forearm, inspecting my skin and the dark blue veins I could see through my flesh. None of the other girls I knew had visible veins, not like these. My parents didn't have them, neither did my brother, nor any of my glamorous, tall, busty cousins with their long, sleek hair and full lips and did I mention their massive boobs? It was vein cancer, I decided — nothing else could explain the cerulean blue of these veins, how close they were to the surface, how they ran all the way up my arm and would appear and disappear across my flat chest. I never told my parents about it and quietly accepted death as I wrote my "Last Willing Testament" on a pink heart-shaped notepad. (This phase never entirely passed. At a dinner party a few years ago, I was seated next to an emergency room doctor. I stuck my arm under her nose and asked, "What does this look like to you?" She said it was nothing, but speaking as someone who once went to a university with a pre-med program, I'm pretty sure I know a little more than she does.)

But even my worst dramatics weren't all that bad. I was still a teenager and prone to typical boundary-pushing. I lied about dates and friends and drinking. I smoked cigarettes and wore poorly applied makeup. I was doing what you're supposed to do when you're young and hateful, and it was all okay because I was home with my mom. She yelled at me with unbelievable bluster, threatened to murder me in such a subtle fashion that "no one will know" or with such flare that "everyone will see." She'd chase me around the house with a wooden spoon, threatening a whipping if I ran my mouth one more time. None of it led to much of anything. I was never in danger. Nothing bad can happen to you if you're with your mom. Your mom can stop a bullet from lodging in your heart. She can prop you up when you can't. Your mom is your blood and bone before your body even knows how to make any.

I have never had to be brave. Bravery is for parents and people who get tattoos in another language or dare to eat pinkish chicken. But my boyfriend, my Hamhock, he has always been brave. It was written somewhere in the skies that he would be made of steel and grit, he would take on every dare or bet, he would hurt himself and brush it off because the brave don't worry about their bodies or their brains. He once got into a bad bike accident that shattered his foot and wrist. He still tried to drive himself to the hospital. At my most self-pitying, I have dreams of drowning in vast bodies of water, my near-dead corpse being dragged back to the surface by the hulking meat of my boyfriend's arms.

So while Hamhock mumbled something to me about how nice the beaches on Ko Phi Phi would be, I felt the plane make an insignificant but intestine-tightening dip before soaring even higher. Hamhock is all the things I am not. He never wanted a life inside. He likes to bike and run and touch and eat and dive headfirst into trouble. (Later on this trip, he would convince me that buying some mysterious snake-fermented wine would be a good idea. We took shots on my birthday. He threw up immediately.) His laugh is high-pitched — like a Pillsbury Doughboy that has fireworks for arms — and I've learned to be wary of it since

it signals some kind of fun and/or threat. But the choice
with him has always been to watch him leave or to pack a
bag and some disinfectant and maybe a pouch of that mal-
aria medication and walk into the unknown, together.

The trip was intended to be restful, I think. It was just
long enough to see a few beaches and temples and eat
some noodles and get drunk four or five times. I knew
two weeks in a foreign country with their weird bugs
and aggressive sunlight would be a challenge. I just didn't
think it would be a catalogue of all my greatest fears.

Spiders scuttling on the ceiling of our hotel room
were the size of my fists. Mystery bugs feasted on my
calves and made my left leg swell so much that I couldn't
walk (at least, not without complaining). I'm afraid of
water, so naturally, several of our destinations were
accessible only by boat. And not real boats with life
jackets and horns but dinky wooden ones with a motor
too big to be supported by a vessel. They looked like
toys that would capsize if you mounted them too
quickly. They sped too fast and would tilt and rock and
splash you with water. The paint was peeling, the metal
was rusted, the seats were barely nailed down. We'd get
too close to other boats and scrape their sides. During
the rides, Hamhock would talk about how much he'd
love a beer; I wanted to see licences and insurance
papers and Thai safety regulations. And while Hamhock
tilted his head back to let the sun wash over his skin,
I clutched any surface of the craft I could as it crashed

down against the water. I'd let out little "eep"s while trying not to look horrified. Now and then, he'd turn to me and ask, "Are you okay?" and I would yell, "YES, THANK YOU, I AM VERY FINE AND CASUAL."

Once we got to Ko Phi Phi Don, Hamhock jumped overboard before we even came to a full stop. He swam around, letting the water cool him down like a playful dolphin. I hung off the side of the boat before letting my body fall in, then flailed towards him and clung to his back like a kinkajou just trying to stay alive long enough to be sent to a nice, temperature-controlled zoo where I'd be guaranteed that the other animals had also been vaccinated.

Later that day, we went snorkelling. I had spent days psyching myself up to swim in open, unregulated waters with choppy waves and salt that rubs itself into all the tiny cuts you didn't know you had all over your body. When we climbed into the boat that would take us to the reef, I quietly prayed for this to go smoothly, for me not just to survive it but to avoid embarrassing myself in front of the other couple joining us. I wore a life jacket in the water like a child too unsure of herself to go into the community pool alone. I saw a reef shark underwater – a vegetarian – and panicked so fiercely that I smashed my knee on a chunk of coral, then worried that the shark would smell the blood and take a sharp right, suddenly deciding he liked the taste of Brown Coward.

Even more pathetic, maybe, is that I actually *can* swim. My mom made me take six years of swimming lessons, in case I somehow risked drowning in landlocked Calgary. She likes to tell the story of my brother, who, the first time he encountered a pool, jumped into the deep end without being able to swim. I, you will not be surprised to hear, never did this.

When we returned to shore, Hamhock and I took a dip in the water – our feet touching the bottom, an imperative for me. But Hamhock pulled me in and lifted me up, threatening to dunk my head under. I kicked and punched until he released me, my head still dry, his body covered in deep scratches from my long nails.

"Were you always like this?" he asked before diving under and not coming up for ten, fifteen seconds, each of them a lifetime for me.

Fear was inherent in our family, but it was magnified by the ever-looming promise of death. As long as I've known him, my dad has always been on alert, either because his father died so young and suddenly or because his mother could have died at any moment. I've only ever known Papa as a man without a father, but I was in my early twenties when Behenji died. Papa cried for a full day, and then took on her fate for himself: "Be good," he told me, "because one day I won't be here."

Mom raised me with an undercurrent of fear beneath her hysterics, but it was only after she lost both of her parents within eleven months of each other that it really vocal cords snap every time you inquired about her mother's health. She didn't even have the energy to fight with me. Once, when she returned home from India jet-lagged and devastated, I presented her with yet another failed math test that my teacher required I get signed. Usually this resulted in Mom screaming about my missed potential, how it was important I become a doctor or a lawyer or an engineer, how I needed to work harder. Instead, she scratched her signature on the top of the page and asked, softly, "What happened here?" I shrugged, and she sank into the couch. I waited by her side, thinking she was gathering the ire to grab me by my collar or to ban me from using the internet for a few days. Nothing came.

Almost a year later, my mother again returned to India, to the two-room house her parents shared. Her mother died. Eleven months later, my Gentle Giant grandfather was gone too. Mom came home from India with his reading glasses and a few pictures. For months, I'd catch her staring out the big window in our living room, her face shiny from crying. I'd ask her what she was thinking about, and she'd let out a big sigh. "Oh, sometimes I look around and I think I've seen my mom. But she's not there." She'd sit upstairs at the makeshift temple she built in their guest room and would weep over her father's memory, her tears falling on his reading glasses, and she'd wipe them off with her little fingers. What was once worth exploring and seeing and tasting and tripping over had now punished her, isolated her in a second country in her third, maybe fourth language. With both her parents gone, there was no one left to soak up that fear, the responsibility of worry. After Papa lost his mother, he got angry enough for the entire family. He sulked, and he raged at bottles that didn't open easily or when the television glitched or when the Wi-Fi felt slower than usual. When Mom lost her parents, she sank into fear. She just wanted everyone to stay home.

We lived three minutes from a Mac's Convenience where I'd go for ten- and twenty-five-cent candies from a bulk bin, but never alone. ("Someone might grab you," Mom would say.) I couldn't go on a sleepover if my friend's mom wasn't home and it was just her dad. ("You can't trust men," something my father – a human man – would say, which I would later learn wasn't entirely untrue.) For years, my hair had to be pulled away from my face and fastened with a scrunchie, as if loose hair said something about loose character. (When my mom prepped my ponytail for a dinner party and a strand hung over my eyes, I asked if I could keep it that way. "What are you, a *teenager*?" she asked, horrified by the prospect of my inevitable aging, dragging the wayward hair into the silvery band. When I became a teenager a few years later, I let my hair hang over my face at all times.)

It was all in the service of keeping their daughter safe, but with the added bonus of making me afraid of nearly everything, external and internal. Boys scared me well into my twenties, and although it was legal in my province to get a driver's licence at fourteen, I waited until seventeen and then only drove once on my own because Papa wanted me to go well below the speed limit (also to stop the car as soon as I saw a yellow light, wherever I was, it almost didn't matter if the light was for my lane, just stop the car and maybe call an ambulance). When I went to Girl Guide camp, I refused to help build a fire by lighting a match because what if I burned my entire fucking arm off? Wouldn't you feel bad then, Supervisor Tara, when you returned me to my mother damaged and charred, you Catholic devil?

I left home right after high school, a few years after my grandparents' deaths, hardly ready to be without my mother. Every cell in me told me not to go, that my parents were right that the rest of the world was gearing up to kill me. Neither of my parents ever told me not to go, but I knew they wanted to. I wanted to stop myself too. When I got into university, Mom smiled meekly and sighed. "I'm happy for you," she said. "But are you sure?" It didn't help that once I did leave, my mother called daily, constantly checking in to see whether I was sick or hurt or destitute or desperate. If I didn't pick up, it merited blind panic and possibly a missing persons report. I started to carry my phone around in my bra just in case "something" happened – that nebulous designation of "something," the vague suggestion that at any point, the world will collapse, and oh, if only I had my phone!

I didn't become afraid of flying until my mother started talking about planes as if they were all doomed Zeppelins. Instead of "Have a nice flight," it was "Call me the second you land." I wasn't nervous around water until a trip to Cuba when she called and warned me to stay away from the ocean: "You'll get arrogant and a wave will come and just get you." (On a different trip, to Greece, I received one foreseen text from her that simply read, "Remember it is SEA.") Papa wouldn't even acknowledge the trip to Cuba at all and instead gave me an eight-day silent treatment. Nothing, it seems, scares you into perpetual fear quite like becoming one of the oldest in your bloodline.

Mom doesn't like it when I fly or take the subway or cross busy intersections. She suggests I avoid eating new things or talking to strangers or getting the flu, because who knows what could kill me? She sends panicked texts when she hears it'll snow in my city, checking in to make sure that I have "enough food and socks." She calls when there's a power outage in a neighbouring town. As a kid, Mom babied me when I had a cough with soups and frozen treats but never mentioned emergency rooms or blood transfusions. Colds didn't concern her until both her parents came down with what seemed like small illnesses that, in the end, killed them. Now, if I sound remotely ill, her first instinct is to demand I take a four-hour flight home so that she can take me to the hospital. Is that too inconvenient? Fine, then she is more than willing to come to me with some clear broths.

Papa would also prefer I stay at home. At this point, he'll settle for anyone's home, not necessarily his own miles away from where I now live. At twenty-two, I went to Ecuador for a week, and the night before I left, my dad sent me an email that wasn't so much a plea for me to be careful as it was a request for me to not do anything, ever.

What was the rationale in choosing the country you are going to. Is it some sort of getting back at me. You know that I will be up for all the period that you will be gone. Your brother did not go anywhere this exotic. What did I do to you. I did exactly what you wanted to do in terms of your post high school education. Is this Hostel that you are going to be safe. Do you have to share bathroom. What other places are you visiting. I know there is nothing I can do except stay up nights and days while you are away. No other kid has done this. Why, why.

May some heavenly force be your protector. I have been rendered speechless. Who are other people going with you. Why could you not visit home for these number of days. You have whole life ahead to go to these places.

He was indeed rendered speechless: as is his wont, he refused to speak to me for a week after I returned, unscathed. "What's in Ecuador?" he asked once he was ready to talk to me again. "Some volcanoes and people who don't speak English. THAT'S ALL."

When you leave the protective wing of your family for the first time, it takes a while before you learn that the only person now tasked with taking care of you is you. For the first year, I drank too much and licked powdered cheese off my fingers for dinner and collapsed on side streets alone, but once I realized that this was my life now, a life without my parents circling me with hair ties ("It's going to get caught in your seatbelt") or plates of protein-rich food ("Your eyes will fall out of your head if you don't eat"), it was up to me to be afraid for me. I lost any real interest in travelling, because the world was a disease-ridden place that would kill you if given the chance. My panic attacks resurfaced – I lived four minutes from campus, but would be late for every class because I just wasn't sure if this was a good day to leave the house. The universe told me it was an inauspicious time.

I now call my parents every day. My dad usually asks the same questions, his barometer of whether it's still okay to let me be on my own: "Are you okay? How are you feeling? Are you weak? You sound weak." Every time he asks me, I want to collapse into him a little more. I want to beg to come home, where I can keep an eye on them, and they can keep their eyes on me. Maybe we won't die if we're constantly looking at each other.

Sometimes when I call I feel my mother's fear and distress so deeply that it scrapes my insides clean. She answers the phone with a weak purr, groaning "Hiiii," as if it's taking all her energy to push air out of her lungs. Ask her how she's feeling and maybe she'll squeeze out, "Oh, I'm okay, just tired." Mom's health always looms over us – over me – thanks to the rheumatoid arthritis in her ribs and her hands and her elbows, the stomach aches, the unexplained chest pains and fainting spells. Every few years, she's taken to the ER or is mounted in the back of an ambulance and I feel the world stop until I know she's home again. One morning when I was in the fifth grade, her blood sugar dipped and she fainted in our living room. I packed my lunch into my backpack while a very nice EMT named Chris took her blood pressure and asked her if she knew where she was. She thought he was her son. (Wishful thinking, maybe. They always wanted him to be a doctor.)

When I first told them about Hamhock, they were livid – he's white and older than the entire solar system and it wasn't someone they chose, so I did them no favours – but while Papa was mad, he put on like he was upset for Mom's sake. "She can barely eat," he told me over the phone, as if this able-bodied woman had become an amoeba overnight. Papa talks about Mom like this a lot, like a weak fawn, largely because she ends up the vessel for all his anxieties too. (It is, indeed, easy for us to think Mom is weak. She absorbs everything from the rest of us, her ungrateful, dissonant family.) She took on the responsibility for being afraid for everyone. And if you spend that much time thinking that something is going to happen to you, it's likely because once in your life, something did, and you just don't want it to happen again.

Though Papa didn't like Hamhock, he often delegated his feelings to Mom: it was poor, sad Mom who couldn't handle this, I needed to behave for her sake. He sometimes talks about her as if she's feeble, but I've known the truth from the first time she threatened to strangle me for disorganizing her Tupperware drawer. ("ALWAYS WITH THE TOPS," she'd say, followed by a Kashmiri curse that, roughly translated, threatens you with actual lightning.)

And she, meanwhile, would call me privately and weep and whine and beg me to make choices that wouldn't upset my father so dramatically. "You know how he gets," she told me. "Now he's going to be miserable around here and who will I talk to if he's so angry?"

But she asks about Hamhock. She checks in on him when he gets a cold, punctuated by demands that we just get married already. She is working on it. She's trying to put her fears on hold, for now. Being afraid of the world, of unknown beasts, only makes you feel alone. Sometimes you just need to get on the plane and hope nothing bad happens.

While our boat slapped against the waves in Ko Phi Phi, I braced myself for every impact, trying to be brave for Hamhock. *What's the worst that could happen?* I thought. *I can swim. Technically. Are there jellyfish in this water? Christ, maybe for our next vacation we can fly directly into the sun's core.*

I felt like I did at twelve on the back of my mom's Sea-Doo when we took summer trips to Kelowna. She always sped too fast for me to feel comfortable, the front of the vehicle going smack-smack-smack against Lake Okanagan. I'd grip my mom's soft belly and she'd laugh, that deep chuckle that rumbles out of her heart, and tell me to stop whining. When we'd return to land, all the other parents would ask me if I'd had fun and I'd grumble and tell them I was never speaking to my mother again. But it wasn't real fear because I was with my mom. Nothing bad happens when you're with your mom.

After we landed from our turbulent flight home, I phoned my mom to let her know I was fine, omitting, of course, all the rickety boat rides and rocky flights and flesh-eating bugs and likely poisonous protein I had eaten. She let out an audible breath and told me she was glad we had a good time. I felt guilty for being gone, for making her anxious despite her own attempts to not imagine the worst. If I was that nervous having fun, I can't imagine how it must have felt to be waiting for me to come home. Why do I keep doing this to her? Why do I let her feel so terrible? Are these trips really worth torturing this woman? That's enough. That's enough of everything.

"Oh," she said. "I forgot to tell you. We're going to Cuba next month."

Though the walls of her house seem to be curling around her, my mom is trying to claw her way out. I can sometimes see her push against whatever her brain is doing to keep her in the house, safe, quiet, sleepy. Sometimes she will talk herself into driving alone in less than ideal weather conditions. Now and then, I can convince her to eat something rapturously unhealthy. I once got her to drink two glasses of white wine and she ended up so drunk that she demanded to know "where the chicken went" and why I "ate all the chicken without asking." There was no chicken in the house. I apologized regardless. It was just nice to see her fall asleep on the couch, upright, mouth still filled with the pasta she had asked me to reheat for her.

She's starting to laugh again when my dad becomes furious over small indignities. He's still anxious about the future, angry about the inevitability of death, angry when he's hungry, angry when he's tired, but Mom just laughs most of it off. I visited them right before they left for Cuba, and sat on their bed watching them pack. They had the same bedspread they had when I was a kid, a white Kutch quilt, pastel pink and green triangles sewn on along with little round mirrors. While my mom packed for St. Thomas when I was in the second grade, I tried to find my reflection warped in those little pieces of glass, tried to figure out how someone could make them so thin that they didn't hurt when you sat on them, and so malleable that they wouldn't break under your weight. Nearly twenty years later, I picked at them all the same while my parents considered taking two bags for a week in Cuba. Two bags each.

"How many pants should I take?" my dad asked.

"One," I said. "It's thirty degrees in Cuba. Why will you need multiple pants?"

"What if we go for dinner?"

"So then you have your one pair of pants."

"But if it rains?"

"It will still be thirty degrees and you will be indoors."

"I don't like being cold."

"It won't be cold, it will be thirty degrees."

"But you don't know that."

"I feel like meteorologists know that."

My dad took three pairs of pants, two shorts, an armload of T-shirts (mostly emblazoned with the logos of pharmaceuticals he used to hawk when he was working), and his go-to vacation outfit: linen pants, sandals, and a muted Tommy Bahama knock-off, with palm trees painted in beige and off-white and light brown.

I watched in awe as they proceeded to stuff suitcases with a five-pound bag of almonds ("I need to have almonds every day and what if they don't have almonds there?"), a 500 mL jug of SPF 60 (have I mentioned that my parents have brown skin?), a "family-sized" bottle of Tylenol with enough pills to kill a small camel, energy bars, three packs of gum, and four ham sandwiches for the four-hour flight. They brought *ham sandwiches* to the place that inspired the *cubano*.

Papa insisted that Mom bring non-perishable chutneys "just in case," while all she took were a few dresses and a bathing suit. Before they even left the house, my father was already telling her that they would not be going anywhere near the ocean and they would never leave the quiet protection of a shaded area. Mom tucked a sun hat and a few books into the remaining nooks of her bag. Papa flicked on the television to watch the news – the third of his four daily doses of television news, where he tsk-tsk-tsks his way through local news at five, local news at six, national news at ten, and international news at eleven, marvelling at the destruction and decay on his doorstep. "I don't even know why I agreed to this in the first place," he said. "What's out there that I don't have at home?" Mom just sighed and rewrapped their sandwiches in T-shirts so they wouldn't get squished. Papa didn't like the idea of being in a foreign bed, in a country that has a blistering sun, near sand that once in your shoes can never be emptied, and away from the routine of my mother making him an egg-white omelette in the morning and my niece swinging by in the early afternoon to pinch and kiss and bite and scream. Papa, the vessel for once; Mom, holding the keys and trying to get him out the door.

I told her that we would all be fine. Nothing bad would happen while they went on vacation for one week. My brother and I are adults, I reminded them, we can take care of ourselves, we know how to survive without our mother. We would call. The world would not crack open just because they took one vacation in more than a decade.

After they would have arrived at their resort in Veradero, they didn't call, but my brother and I assumed they were eager to start their vacation. The day after, we still heard nothing, but guessed that Wi-Fi was hard to find. Hamhock, my latchkey man, took more relief in his in-laws taking a nice vacation than I did, suggesting they were probably busy drinking and vacationing. "It'll be good for them," he said, so relaxed by their departure that he nearly fell asleep while I expressed my concern.

By the third day, I was in a full panic. They hadn't answered any emails, or turned on their phones, or tried to contact us. Neither I nor my brother had bothered to take down their flight number to make sure the plane landed on time. All we had was the hotel name, with a front desk that spoke exclusively Spanish. With the exception of their trips to India, where they'd send frequent emails, it was the longest I had gone without speaking to them.

"I'm sure they're fine," Hamhock said. "They're on vacation. Let them go on vacation." But how are you supposed to relax when the people who taught you to be afraid of the world, to be alert, to be suspicious, have vanished without a trace and haven't even bothered to let you know that, no, they did not get careless and a wave didn't just come and "get" them? My stomach churned out bile for the remainder of their vacation, and I hoped that they were, in fact, staying out of the sun and far from the ocean and at a safe distance from strangers. This is how these stories start, you know. Someone you love goes on a vacation somewhere relatively safe – my parents have invented this story for me countless times – and then they aren't heard from for a few days too long, and soon their bodies are found mangled on the underside of a cruise ship. *This is how it starts.*

But that is rarely how it ends. My mom texted me when they returned, and I had fully unhinged by then. My brain had planned their funeral and I was already trying to figure out how to tell my brother that I did not want to sell their house because I didn't want anyone else living in our old home.

"INTERESTING HOW YOU THOUGHT IT WAS ACCEPTABLE TO NOT CALL ANYONE FOR NINE DAYS," I texted back to her. "HOPE YOU HAD A GREAT TIME, I AM FURIOUS WITH YOU AND AM NEVER SPEAKING TO YOU AGAIN."

Mom said she was sorry and asked me to call her in the evening so she could tell me about their trip. Apparently they spent nine blissed-out days on the beach. She read a few books and my father tolerated going near the water. Mom patiently listened to me yell at her for forty minutes.

Everything does, usually, turn out to be okay. Mom says this to me all the time now that her fear doesn't swallow her whole, often when I feel like the world won't do what I say. "You know everything always works out," she says. "It always ends up okay." She's right: no real tragedy has occurred, and our family is otherwise quite fortunate.

Death has always been an inevitability, but never one that came before we could prepare for it.

But I know something will come. Something always does. It came for Mom when it took her parents. It came when she lost touch with her brother while they were in their fifties, an unexplained but severe estrangement. It came for Papa when his father died in his sleep. It came for him when his mother started to lose her mind and would disrobe in his brother's living room. It came again when she died. It will come for me, in one way or another, taking my parents, or my brother, or my niece, or, more pressingly, Hamhock.

For now, our age difference is a cute oddity, a funny thing about our relationship that we make light of. But he takes blood pressure medication and will likely die before I turn sixty. I'm staving off this fear. I don't want to play with it right now. "I'm healthier than you," he'll remind me when I worry about his death. "Besides, when it's time to die, it's time." This is of flimsy comfort: unknown forces do not give a shit if your boyfriend is technically in great shape, they will kill him regardless. Sometimes when he's sleeping, I pull on his hair to make sure it's still strong, poke his face to see if he'll swat at me, if he still has his reflexes. Then I can relax. But whatever it is, it will come, and if I can't prevent it, at least I can stay home where it's safe, where I know it's safe, where it's as safe as I can possibly make it.

I let go of my grudge two days after my parents came back from Cuba. I told Hamhock they were fine, that he was right, he's always right. My blood pressure dipped and I got my appetite back. I asked him to rub my back. He shook his head and laughed while I crawled into his lap. "Of course they're fine," he said. "I mean, what exactly were you expecting?"

Papa <papa@gmail.com>, November 30, 2012
You act like I did nothing for you
like you were raised by wolves.

Scaachi <sk@gmail.com>, November 30, 2012
When's my birthday?

Papa <papa@gmail.com>, November 30, 2012
I don't need to answer that.

Size Me Up

——

A mong the many unfair stereotypes lodged against women – small hands, delicate fingers, weak arms, poisonous knees – is the belief that we all love shopping. There is nothing all women like, except maybe television shows where other women scream at each other or have long discussions promoting the demise of the modern man so that we can all live in some utopian future where we can procreate on our own and can finally stop pretending that any of us appreciate having the thin, eerily soft skin of a testicle in our mouths. But shopping is a strange thing to attribute to a specific gender. What about it could be so intrinsically satisfying?

I don't like shopping. In movies that depict a futuristic dystopia, people tend to wear uniforms in a single colour, usually a metallic onesie with a high neck and gender-neutral panelling in the front. I am fine with this. I look great in silver and gold.

Shopping reveals the id in all of us. At blowout sales, I am ready to cold-cock other women also trying on size 10 work-appropriate cocktail dresses that hide their shame (upper arms) while promoting their glory (elegant pinkies and/or pillow-butt). In the changing room, attempting to shove your misshapen body into the size you think you should be rather than the size you are usually leads to some form of weeping while screaming, "IT'S FINE, I'LL JUST WEAR A BAG OF FLOUR AROUND MY BODY UNTIL I DEHYDRATE ENTIRELY AND CAN DIE IN PEACE." Opening your closet to find that you hate every item of clothing you have ever bought is a specific circle of hell: hanger after hanger of poly-cotton blend T-shirts, all with thick layers of deodorant crusted on the armpits, every skirt ironed so poorly it's on the verge of unravelling if you swivel too fast in it, your shoes just leather hunks you force your bunions into.

But despite this hatred of shopping, I have faith in clothing, in its ability to transform you into something or someone better. At our cores, we are all swirling masses of infectious disease, pulsating orbs of pus, moist tubes filled with piss and shit. But maybe if we put on a nice suit or one of those giant statement necklaces that suggest we have more money than we do, someone else will think us clean enough to touch, to go to dinner with, to greet without flinching, to introduce to their parents.

That is why we go shopping. To touch even the tip of our humanity.

Around the age of ten, I gained a significant amount of weight, the kind that family members stop referring to as "cute" or "baby weight" and start referencing with a heavy sigh. There was, in reality, nothing wrong with my weight, but I was too young and too insecure (a lethal combination) to know that. So I did what I thought I should: I hid my rapidly developing body. I started wearing B.U.M. Equipment sweatpants and long-sleeved heat-locking tops — both items were perhaps utilitarian in the winter, but tended to turn my person into a walking, sweating radiator by June. Shopping was my mother's game. She would return from stores that sold clothes exclusively for hikers with a wagonful of wool socks and dungarees for her puberty-stricken daughter. Nothing I owned fit anymore, and I didn't trust that buying the right clothes could make me feel better about the way my hips had widened or my arms had softened or my neck now had ridges running across it as if I were an old tree and these were my rings.

At the time, I claimed my style was some kind of feminist protest: "I don't need to look like every other girl. Why should I have to dress up when guys can wear whatever they want?" I listened to Avril Lavigne and recited the lyrics as if they were my own thoughts; I watched CNN because I didn't want to be a frivolous teen; I had crushes on adult men like Jon Stewart and Rahm Emanuel and hot dads at the mall with salt-and-pepper hair and Palm Pilots. But in truth, I just didn't know if I was allowed to look like a "cute girl" if my body was bigger than the other girls I knew, if my skin was darker, if I was more sullen than sugar. I hid in muted drapery hoping no one would notice or, better yet, they would assume I was just a very tough, genderless sphere.

This crumbled by the time I was eleven: a well-meaning woman at my mother's Jenny Craig meeting told her what a precious son she had. I was wearing a baseball cap with the Coca-Cola logo emblazoned on the front, a red puffy vest, and grey sweatpants. It was July. It was embarrassing to be mistaken for a boy. Not a girl with masculine tendencies, not a girl rejecting traditional gender roles, but a boy. I was being defined by my clothing instead of transformed by it. This was the same year I discovered *Lord of the Rings* weenie Orlando Bloom, a crush that would last twenty-four months and spawn more than one fan club. (My brother was the only member, and only by force.) Boys don't like girls in promotional hats, and I wanted boys to like me. I started growing my hair out, and asked my mom to take me shopping. I wanted to dress like a girl, and not just a pretty girl but a hot girl, that poor definition of whatever makes a woman worth looking at, worth touching. At least, from a teenage boy's perspective. Clothes, the right clothes, could make me – even me! – hot.

Unfortunately, my tastes differed drastically from my mother's. My interests were swaying towards T-shirts with hilarious and racy sayings paired with elastic-waist-banded jeans. I wanted to try on belly tops and white belts with big silver bolts! My mom suggested matching stretchy pants and long-sleeved tops with watercolour wolves standing near the reflection of the moon in a calm river, T-shirts with little frogs posed on 3D lily pads, flowing Indian tunics that I could tell were clearly not "English" clothes, as we called them, ones in jewel tones and gold stitching that screamed, "MY MOTHER IS AN IMMIGRANT, WE ONLY EAT OFF METAL PLATES." She'd hold them up and say, "They look so nice!" and I'd say, "They're itchy!" and she'd say, "How?" and I'd furiously rub the sequins against my skin until I flashed red bumps and then say, "SEE?"

A particular fight between my mother and me broke out in the women's aisle at Walmart the summer before I started middle school, when I found a royal blue shirt with "IF IT WEREN'T FOR BOYS, I WOULDN'T EVEN GO TO SCHOOL" scrawled across the front in harsh yellow. This was a completely false statement for me to support: I wrote extra-credit English essays, joined the school paper, and wept for weeks when my grade-six yearbook failed to print my "Future Goals" next to my school photo, worried that everyone would think I was a purposeless hack. I was afraid of the boys who went to my school, all of whom did not like me and were prone to calling me a faggot. But I felt that if I got this shirt, I could transform myself at my new school. I would be cool and elusive and one of those types people refer to as "chill." What does that even mean? I still have no idea, but I wanted it, and even now, as a tense, uncomfortable adult, I forevermore aim to be "chill."

I had the whole scene planned out: I would walk into school wearing that shirt, along with a set of earrings from Claire's, the ones shaped like lightning bolts to really bring out the yellow in the shirt. I'd pair it with my floor-length patchwork denim skirt with a little Union Jack on the pocket – I did not know the flag's country of origin, but it's not like there was a class I could take at school to teach me junk like flags or stuff. I would encircle my eyes with thick black liner, all the way around, elevating myself from mousy girl to sex-raccoon. Graham, the boy I had the hots for, would really see me for the first time. Not as the girl he once tackled in flag football, but as the *woman* he once tackled in flag football. I would pull my glasses off and the transformation would be complete. *Who is this girl?* everyone would ask. *It's me,* I'd say. The crowd would gasp in amazement and I would have a million friends and be very thin and rich and filled with an embarrassment of sexual energy for a thirteen-year-old.

While I was concocting this elaborate fantasy in Walmart, my mom was explaining to me why she wouldn't be buying the shirt. "That's inappropriate," she whispered, as if the words themselves were sinful. My mother had a tendency to slip into outrage and shock as a first reaction to anything, and the lower her voice dropped, the more she was disappointed in me. I could barely hear her. "It's not even long enough to cover your tummy!" she said, pulling me towards a row of long-sleeved T-shirts that said "Glam!" in different colours.

We settled on a short-sleeved number with glittery navy vinyl lettering that proclaimed "I'm not perfect, but I'm so close it scares me!" Even though I loved the shirt (so clever, so quietly smart, so, dare I say, *elegantly subversive*), I raged at my mom for weeks. She claimed that shirts like the royal blue one were intended for women like my twenty-year-old cousin and not for pudgy middle-schoolers. But what twenty-year-old is shopping in the girls' section at Walmart, *Mother*? It got worse a few days after classes started, when my arch-nemesis, Stephanie, wore the shirt I'd wanted, getting an obscene amount of negative male attention. I stomped all the way home that afternoon. That was supposed to be *my* negative male attention.

This thinking – finding an outfit that I believe will revolutionize my very existence – is a repeated one of failure throughout my life. There was the pair of faux-leather red peep-toe pumps in 2006, the high-waisted oatmeal-coloured wide-legged trousers of 2008, the black-sequined bolero of 2009, the skin-tight cerise knock-off Hervé Léger "this New Year's Eve is gonna be amaaaaaziiiiiing" bandage dress of 2011 that I still own and pull out from my closet now and then to remind myself of what I cannot be. I still remember my favourite outfit from the tenth grade: a mint-green V-neck lace top, dark-wash boot-cut jeans, and black-and-teal-butterfly Mary Jane kitten heels. I wore that outfit for every major occasion: when I wanted Drew to ask me out (he did not), when I wanted to ace a math exam (I did not), when I wanted to be noticed by an attractive guest speaker (I was not). Despite this piss-poor batting average, I felt a renewed sense of potential every time I put it on. Today, something good has to happen.

Nearly a decade after that outfit stopped being a staple in my wardrobe, I yet again fell into the trap of believing cloth could be revolutionary. Walking through Toronto's financial district, I passed a clothing chain known for simple skirts, blouses, blazers, and a terrible roll-on perfume that burned my neck. It was also the second (and last) retail job I ever had, when I was nineteen and living in my cousin Angie's basement beside her husband's table saw, which he used to make her hand-carved wizard wands. I was at least twenty years younger than the clientele that came into the store, I hardly made enough money to buy the $90 cocktail-casual dresses on the racks, and I managed to be twenty minutes late for every shift. I wasn't fired, per se, but when I left my section of the store to reapply my $4.50 lipstick and a drunk man managed to swipe $800 of merchandise from the store without being detected, I nobly offered not to return for my next shift.

But that was years ago, and I felt a twinge of self-satisfaction in going back as a customer. So much of my life had changed since I had worked there: I wasn't a teenager anymore, I had my own apartment, I had paid my taxes at least once, I bought shoes in real stores instead of waiting for my older cousins to tire of theirs. The store was little more than a reminder of how far I had progressed in a few short years. *Help me with these buttons, shopgirl*, I imagined saying, *for I am an important woman. I own a microwave.*

That said, the real reason I entered the store was far more practical than ego. It was the dead of summer, some thirty-five degrees Celsius, and I am a soggy woman even in the most forgiving conditions. Standing outside the store, I was already sweating in new and interesting parts of my body, and if I didn't get into a building colder than the surface of the moon, my makeup would start bleeding and I'd look like a wax figurine inside a clay oven.

I walked in, relishing the blast of cool air, and immediately saw Aaliyah. She had trained me when I worked there but was now the store manager and still as tall, stately, and glamorous as I remembered her being when I was nineteen. Best of all: she didn't seem to recognize me.

I rummaged through sales rack after sales rack, tossing aside shirts that I knew would cling in the wrong places, colours that brought out the sallow tint of my complexion, and the one-piece jumpers because, inexplicably, adult women were wearing jumpers in droves, and I never figured out how all of them managed to pee while wearing them. I was older, more mature, I had learned some important lessons.

But like most of my shopping trips, I grew frustrated quickly. There was little in my size, and the few things that were listed as an 8 or a 10 were really cut for someone who was a 4 or a 6. Just the thought of forcing my wide hips through trousers or my boulder shoulders through a T-shirt felt like more pain than it was worth.

And yet, on my way out, I found it: the *thing*. A black-and-white fall skirt that I knew would look perfect on me. It was soft wool, but in a slimming cut, and hit just below the knee. It would be perfect for work, or for going out after work, or maybe I would wear it with a big floppy hat and a trench coat at Parisian cafés, waiting for a parcel from a mysterious stranger. (I am Carmen Sandiego in this fantasy, like I am in most of my non-sexual, non-food-related fantasies.) I held my breath, turning it over to see the price and the size: it was on sale, and it was a size 8.

It's happening, I thought. The item, the big item that changes the way I dress and thereby changes the way I am as a person. It's not just a skirt; it's the entry fee for a better existence. I would exude a new confidence, it would smooth out the wrinkles in my body, it would hide all the ways I have disappointed and failed people in the past. While wearing it, women would approach me and beg me to tell them where I got it. I would act coy and wink to the camera (in this version of the fantasy, I am perpetually in a commercial; don't worry about it) and say something like, "I'll never tell" or "Oh, just something I picked up." People would see me on the street, shoving fistfuls of Teddy Grahams into my mouth on the way to the podiatrist, and they would think, "Boy, that lady sure does have her life together."

That's a lot of pressure for something on sale for $24.99.

Aaliyah led me to a changing room, complimenting me on my choice. I locked the door and looked at myself in the mirror, taking a deep breath. This could be it. I peeled the shorts off my sweating skin and stepped into the skirt. It slid up my body, resting on my waist, and I pulled the zipper up towards the lord. It didn't just fit. No, it did more than that. It melded to my body, beautifully, as if it had been cut specifically for me, to mask and smooth and elevate. I would be better in this skirt. The dream was happening! I had the all-knowing smile, my hair was suddenly more luxurious, I felt thinner, more acceptable. I was a better woman. Girls who had been mean to me in high school would see me in this skirt and think, "Is that Scaachi?" and I'd say, "YOU BET IT IS, YOU DUMB BITCH" and then punch all their boyfriends in the teeth. (I have not thought this fantasy through; just let me have this.)

Conflated imaginings aside, I did look pretty good. I walked out of the changing room to vamp in front of people paid to tell me I looked great. The skirt was a little warm for the summer, but who cares, I'd wear it when fall came. I did one more spin in front of Aaliyah and her co-workers before feeling a thick droplet of sweat fall from my brow onto my eyelash. I was overheating in my perfect skirt, so I headed back into the changing room.

My hands were sweating too much to grasp the zipper in the back. I wrapped a T-shirt around my fingers to get a grip, but it wouldn't budge. I sucked in, gathering the fabric, and tried to tug the zipper down. No luck. I struggled like this for a good fifteen minutes, the changing room lights feeling more like an interrogation lamp, sweat pooling in the dimples above my ass, my hair matted to my face.

I had fallen into this trap before, so many times. Years before this, I went through a phase of buying clothes only from vintage stores: beautiful dresses and skirts that required real care and attention that I wasn't willing to give to another person, never mind a chiffon gown. They had no elastic, bled colour wherever you sat, with zippers that rusted and fell apart like rotting teeth. My favourite purchase was a cocktail dress: it was a simple blood-red shift that came with a layer that slipped on top, a long peplum type that made my waist look small. I wore it too often, too many places. Paired with irrational brown heels, I wore it to school with my hair done and red lipstick, as if at any moment, someone would rush into my JRN 121 class and say, "Help, I am a very wealthy lawyer and I need an extremely well-dressed young woman to join me on my yacht for a party that might have some influence in making me partner. Also, I am looking for a wife to politely ignore but who may spend my money freely and maintain multiple quiet affairs with my handsome co-workers. You look ironed. Are you interested?"

But I didn't know how to care for the dress. It had been made in the '50s for a woman an inch or two thinner than me, so I was already testing the tensile strength of the seams. I hand-washed it in cold water – isn't that what you do with delicate items? – the dress bleeding out its red colour, fading it slightly. But it also shrank, somehow, now only reaching halfway down my thigh. It was too much for school (oh, *now* it's too much) but fine for any other occasion. Yes, it was so tight on my ass and hips that I couldn't sit down in it, but that just meant I'd wear it to run errands. When my cell phone broke and I needed to get it repaired, I wore my favourite dress and my brown heels to the mall. While the rep explained the damage to my phone ("Unfortunately, we can't replace any phones that might have been dropped in liquids or foods, and I can see some marinara in the headphone jack"), I felt the dress tear right between my butt cheeks. There was no seam there, but certainly some considerable tension.

I pressed the flap of the top layer of the dress down over the new hole and tried to scurry out. Before I left, the rep stopped me to say, "By the way, I really like your outfit." I kept the dress just in case my body one day became drastically different and I could maybe fit in it again. After, of course, repairing the six-inch-long tear in the back.

But back in the changing room, I was reaching peak anxiety. I tried pulling the skirt over my head (alas, my waist is smaller than my shoulders, a problem I did not consider until I almost got my arms stuck in the skirt as well), then considered tearing the zipper and telling Aaliyah that it broke while I was trying to disrobe.

But I didn't want to ruin such a good item. Maybe it was salvageable. Maybe I could still be the woman I felt I could be. My only options were to ask Aaliyah to help me out of the skirt, or to wear it out of the store, making me the only idiot sweating in a wool skirt in thirty-degree heat who wasn't also handing out pamphlets that read "Have You Made Peace With Your God?" Sometimes zippers move when you rub a candle on them. I could run outside and yell, "DOES ANYONE HAVE A CANDLE? IT'S AN EMERGENCY." That would be fine. I considered a secret third option in that changing room, one where I would type out a quick suicide note on my phone and then use a fabric belt to fashion a trendy noose.

Whatever the decision, I needed to make it fast, since soon my whole body would be covered in my salty, sticky shame-sweat.

I left the changing room and tapped Aaliyah on the shoulder, hoping she wouldn't notice my entire face was glistening.

"That really does look great on you," she said, giving me that wide smile I had seen her give to so many customers before.

"I'm stuck," I said.

I turned around, my rear towards her, and she tried

the zipper herself. She tried bunching the fabric to get a better grip. "Suck in," she said, pulling more and more of the skirt towards her. She called over her co-worker to help. She, too, couldn't manage. "It's so weird," she said. "It's like the skirt is caught on nothing." No, nothing except my own ego and humiliation. I flew too close to the sun with this skirt. I thought it would transform my life. I thought it would make me better.

A third employee came over and tried to use a pin to pull the zipper's teeth apart. She spent a full minute just shaking my hips, as if she was trying to will me to a smaller size so the skirt would slide off. (Admittedly, a minute may not sound like a long time, but ask a loved one to shake the lower half of your body vigorously for an entire minute, and then ponder how long those sixty seconds feel like.)

The employees turned to each other and discussed what to do next. "We could rip out the zipper and then sew it back on?" "Do you think she can pull it over her head, or, no, no, her shoulders are too wide." "What if we just cut her out?"

That last one was the ultimate nightmare. If you are a woman reading this, you know this to be true: the possibility of getting stuck in a garment at a store where the employees have to cut you out of it is the beginning of the end of your life. It's like the saddest version of a C-section, where the baby is just a half-naked lady with no dignity.

"Yeah," Aaliyah said to her cohorts. "Grab the scissors. We have to cut her out." It was like listening to three surgeons decide you needed to be sliced in half, thinking you're unconscious and can't hear them.

Two women held the skirt to my hips, pressing me into the wall of the changing room hallway. I could see my reflection in the mirror, my face now drenched with sweat. From the outside, I looked like I was being hazed by a group of women far too old to be welcoming in new pledges. All I was focused on, however, was not exposing my entire lower half to whoever may have walked into the store during this ordeal. I said a silent goodbye to my beloved skirt, the garment that was supposed to change me but instead reminded me that, no, you are what you are, even if you remember to iron your clothes.

"Okay, hold still," Aaliyah said. This was an intimate moment for us. Her face was closer to my butt than anyone's had been in, oh, hours. We were like sisters now.

While the other two women flanked me and held the skirt up, Aaliyah pulled the fabric away from my body and started making small cuts. "I don't want to cut you," she said, but at that point, I welcomed any distraction from the sweat gathering on my back. Like tiny, resplendent pools of my greatest fear come to life.

The sound that's made when one cuts a perfectly useful item of clothing is almost painful, especially when it's one that you have fallen in love with. All those hems and seams and stitches destroyed so easily. It's the same feeling, I imagine, that would come if you baked and iced a cake, only to drop it on the way to a birthday.

But the sound that's made when someone, say, cuts an item of clothing they weren't supposed to cut is criminal. It's the dying scream of someone you love. It is the final whisper of your pride. It is the quietest slap in the face you will ever feel.

When she made her final cut, I turned to Aaliyah to thank her — maybe I would make a joke about how we had worked together, how I had let all that merchandise just walk out of the store and here I was, doing it again — but all the colour had drained from her face. She had sliced right through my underwear, leaving me exposed like either a confused surgery patient or a very physically confident crazy person.

It was an honest mistake on her part. I hope. I was wearing one of those 1999-esque whale tails that were popular among high school girls trying to attract boys with the forbidden fruit of tiny underwear. It wasn't so much clothing as it was thickly woven black floss, hanging out inside the crevices of my garbage body.

Aaliyah wordlessly ushered me back into the changing room, then gave me the scissors, saying I could cut myself out further if I needed to. I tore the skirt right in half, looking at what was hanging off me in the mirror. One hip, wrapped in an elastic band like a still-raw roulade, the other naked except for a thick thread swinging, purposelessly, by my side. I started to get dressed, trying to see if I could tie my underwear back together or maybe cinch it with the hair elastic I had around my wrist. Instead, I opted to just stuff myself back into my denim shorts.

I handed Aaliyah the remains of the skirt and the scissors, apologizing for destroying a perfectly good item of clothing. "Oh, it's okay," she said, "it happens," though she didn't clarify to whom else it had ever happened. I bought that trendy noose belt to compensate. And then, of course, as I shuffled out of the store, I heard Aaliyah proclaim with great zeal, "Oh my god, I just remembered where I know her from!"

The nightmare was over, but I still had to sulk home in a heat wave, my clothes soaked from sweat, my underwear hanging on by a single thread. And if you have never experienced the sensation of your naked labia rubbing up against freshly washed denim as you manoeuvre through a subway car with broken air conditioning, you have had more than your fair share of luck in this life.

I returned home the way I always do, with no renewed outlook on life and no magic garment to change the way I am. I hung my new belt (still never worn) in my closet among all the other clothes that I had, at one point, bought in order to improve my life. All of them had failed me because clothes just can't improve you. They can't make you feel better about yourself for more than a few minutes, they can't make you a better person than you are, because they're all just things you bought at the mall, that you then ruin with pizza sauce stains, that you then wear to bed or use to polish jewellery. I still go through the same routine where I shop to save my soul instead of just to cover my ass, and it typically ends the same way. That maxi-dress from nine months ago didn't cure me of hating the width of my hips. The earrings from two years ago don't distract me from how I feel about my uneven hairline. And the skirt Aaliyah cut me out of would not have made me feel any better about how quickly sweat can puddle at the nape of my neck. I wonder, sometimes, if my mom had just bought me that shirt from Walmart, if I would have been saved all this nitpicking I do to my own body: maybe I would be kinder to my arms and my neck, maybe I wouldn't worry about what people might be saying about my baby hair.

But probably not. There will be something else to make me feel bad, inching up towards all the things I currently feel bad about, and no crop top made by small, underpaid, foreign hands can cure me – or you. Clothes are ephemeral: they fall apart in the wash, you lose them at a friend's house, they rip and crumble and go out of style. You'll forget about them and buy new ones and then start the cycle again. But your insecurities, the ones that make you go hunting for something to make you feel better, to love yourself more, to give you a renewed sense of self or greater esprit – don't you even worry. Those will last you a lifetime.

Papa <papa@gmail.com>, November 17, 2015

Do not forget to pack a towel in your suitcase in case.

Scaachi <sk@gmail.com>, November 17, 2015

In case of *what*?

Papa <papa@gmail.com>, November 17, 2015

It is India, the land of Sadhus, snake charmers, multizillioniars, charlatans, extremely happy destitute so be prepared for anything. So pack your towel.

Fair and Lovely

———

L ike farts and the incorrect retellings of classic litera-
ture, racism is a lot cuter when it comes out of a little
girl. When we first told my niece, Raisin, that we would
all be going to India for a wedding, she scrunched her face
up and said she didn't want to go. "Everyone there is
poooooor," she told us. "And Indians smell bad." She hadn't
yet connected that, to begin with, half of her family is
Indian, and more importantly, she is half Indian. She was
only five at the time, young enough that everyone just
rolled their eyes at her and knew she would be swayed
by her first fresh electric-orange jalebi.

But it bothered me. Almost a year earlier, she'd said

something else about how she didn't like Indians. It was one of only a few times I've yelled at her, and she went quiet and her eyes were glassy. "Sorry," she said, hugging me around the waist. "Don't be mad at me, Boo." She calls me Boo, the truncation of Bua, or paternal aunt, and I call her Raisin because her skin wasn't always so porcelain white. She came out purple, wrinkled, furious – like so many, regardless of race.

When Raisin was born, her eyes were a cloudy blue. "They'll get darker," Mom told me. "They usually do." She was fair-skinned, even fairer than her dad – my brother – who has the surprising complexion of a standoffish vampire. She had less hair than any of her brown family members had at birth. All of this was a victory to us, to my mom, to me. I quietly hoped her eyes would stay blue, that she would keep these recessive features from the white half of her family. When she looked at me, I could see her pupils, and I remembered how that was such a luxury when I was a kid. In the fifth grade, our teacher made us stand nose to nose so we could see what happens to the human pupil when lights are turned on and off. My partner was Bryn, a white girl with baby blues, and I watched as her irises shrank and grew. "I can't see yours at all," Bryn said. "You're like a shark." Raisin would not be a shark.

We were less pleased, then, with her nose, wide and squished – very Indian, very ours. "Maybe it'll get smaller?" Mom said. But no, we knew she was stuck with our nose. "I wonder if we could put one of those black binder clips on it," Papa said. "Make it a bit thinner." But she was perfect the way any tiny body that enters your family is perfect. We all wanted to touch her head and smell her hair and carry her around like a little doll. Papa would hold her in one hand and with the other pull apples down from the sour apple tree in the backyard. My dad, his olive skin darkening in the sun, his thick beard and hooked nose contrasted with Raisin's little face, her pink skin, her blue eyes. (They did, indeed, get darker, and now they look like blue Warheads. Her skin, though, is as pearly as ever.)

In India, I meet Raisin and the rest of my extended family at the train station, since they had been touring the country for a week before I landed. We are there for my cousin Sweetu's wedding, the latest in a long line of my generation to accept a modernized arrangement. Chacha, my dad's younger brother, picks me up from the airport and takes me to meet everyone, with Raisin and twenty or so of my other family members spilling out from the station entrance. Raisin is wearing leggings with knock-off emojis and a T-shirt that says "UNDERCOVER NINJA." Her light brown hair is tied in a French braid but frizzed around her face, like a halo. She launches from her father's arms into mine, squeezes me around the neck, and gives me her requisite, "Hi, Boo."

"Did you have fun on the train?" I ask her.

"Yeah, but my tummy hurt." She is clutching a Sprite bottle and has that sickly look of a small body that has been hurling from motion sickness.

The last time we came to India as a family, I was ten. My brother had orange-frosted tips and was getting his undergrad, my mother's parents were alive, as was my dad's mother. Raisin wasn't even a concept yet. We took the train during that trip, and I too emerged feeling queasy and needing to be held.

This trip is different for obvious reasons, but it is always the same town, it is always December when we come, it is always twenty degrees, cooler since we are far north. My aunts still greet me by rubbing my face and telling me that I look like their mother, so beautiful, so fair. Chacha calls me fat and then laughs so hard that he starts coughing. (I call him old and he forms his hand into a butcher knife, making little chops at my neck.) Nothing has changed, and yet I am holding a little white body and people passing by are looking, because she so clearly cannot belong to us. She looks so out of place here, even next to the other little kids she is related to. She brushes her fingers through my hair and asks, "Boo, did you bring me any chocolate?" She never notices when people are looking.

Calgary was a city of just over a million when I was growing up there. It's split into four clearly divided quadrants: northwest, southwest, northeast, southeast. We lived in the southwest: a predominantly Caucasian neighbourhood with plenty of kids and schools and grocery stores. We were

one of a few non-white families in the area. The northeast, comparatively, is rife with immigrants, particularly
South Asian immigrants. You can move to northeastern
Calgary and get by speaking Hindi or Punjabi only. It was
a long drive for us, though, so we visited the area spar-
ingly. I knew they were my people, but it didn't feel like
it. I was pushing against any first-generation narrative,
while all the people in that area were seemingly proud of
it. Aunties wore salwars to go grocery shopping, and little
kids had those silver or gold bangles we were all given
at birth. My brother has always worn a gold chain with
a pendant that has his initials, but he tucks it under his
collar. In the northeast, the boys wore them outside their
basketball jerseys. We were different from them, and I
was determined to keep us different. Every piece of gold
jewellery ever given to me was hidden in my dresser; I
refused to wear any of it because it made me feel I was
being marked as an Other. (I now wear all of it, sometimes
at the same time, a signal to other Others that I'm an
Other too.) Immigrant parents, when they first move to
North America, push towards whiteness, towards assimi-
lation, to survive and thrive. Naturally, their children do
too for the first half of their lives. This usually tips the
other way, but before we're taught anything, we're taught
to hide.

My friends had white names – Jennifer, Kayla, Kellie,
Molly, Kirsten – names my parents made fun of because
what do those names even mean? A loaded question,

considering the name they gave me barely makes sense to other brown people. When we were in India in the early aughts, Chacha told me that Kayla, or kela, means "banana" in Hindi, and when I took that information back to my friend, we laughed for a solid school year. I had a funny name, and teachers and the parents of other kids always asked: "Where are you from?" I learned fast that the correct answer wasn't "I take the E bus and I'm the second to last stop and that's where I live," but rather "My parents are Indian immigrants." With that answer, their faces would light up and they'd say, "Oh, I hear India is amazing! Does your mom make curry?" Then I would shrug and say, yeah, sure, I guess she does, but isn't that like me asking if your mom boils water?

My race didn't seem like a problem until 9/11, or at least, I never noticed a difference beyond forgettable microaggressions. I watched the towers come down while pulling my socks up in the living room, getting ready for school. Mom sat stock-still, watching in horror, and I remember this only because it was the first time she wasn't rushing me to catch the bus. She sat in the living room on the coffee table, a wooden spoon held aloft, her face frozen in fear. When we got to school, my fifth-grade teacher made us sit around her in a circle and tried to explain what had happened, but mostly asked us to give her our impressions. It boiled down to some "bad guys" taking over a plane. It was like a *Die Hard* plotline, and the only thing that was out of the ordinary was that our teacher wanted to discuss the news, which we would have otherwise ignored. Buildings fell all the time, wars happened. I understood the news as a dark thing to watch. I didn't worry.

But the older kids get, the more context they have about the world, the better they are at putting words to sentiments, and holy shit, are those sentiments ever racist. At a day camp the following summer, I tried to sit with a group of girls I was desperate to be friends with. Their ringleader was a few years older than us, and she was impressive. After all, her cousin was a backup dancer for Britney Spears. (There was absolutely no way to verify this, but I recall thinking that she looked vaguely Hawaiian and so did the dancer so I just chalked it up to something too ridiculous to lie about.) I followed them around for a few days during activities—running in circles, throwing ourselves on padded mats, unstructured hair-braiding time—until I steeled myself to sit with them for lunch. My mom always packed me "white" food, things that wouldn't be "embarrassing." Sandwiches, apples (gross), Rice Krispies, juice boxes, Fruit Roll-Ups. Once, Kayla brought split-pea soup and was teased so relentlessly that I hugged my mom extra tight that evening for never packing me khichdi, even if I did love it. So that day I brought my lunch bag and sat down in the grass with them. But one girl turned to me, flipping her long brown hair over her shoulder, and asked, "Why are you sitting with us?"

"Why not?" I said.

"You're brown."

Ohh, I thought, *so this is what it is.* This was the difference felt but rarely spoken. This was why certain girls just didn't want to be friends with me, it's why certain parents looked at me for too long. It's why everyone wanted to know where I was from. I was *brown.* Calgary didn't have a huge black population at the time, but I knew one black girl in kindergarten and I knew that was the word for her. There was a Chinese girl in the first grade and she called herself "Asian" so I knew that was the name for that. But for us, I never named it. Papa told me we were Kashmiri, which was good, because we were from the north. He told me we were of the Brahmin caste, we were descendants of pundits, literally meaning we were smart and educated and worthy, cultural history that wasn't necessarily true but was certainly felt. He never outright mentioned that we were also some of the fairest in the country, and how our privilege was largely related to the sheer dumb luck of being lighter, but I'd figure that out soon enough. Papa talked about us as though we were the best India had to offer.

That, however, doesn't matter when you just want to get through junior high. Some boys brought me a deodorant stick to help mask my "natural" curry scent. In grade eight, Joshua, a guy whose main vocation was eating erasers, called me Osama bin Laden's cousin. I took out my gold ruby hoops — the same ones my grandmother had worn — because they felt too obvious. I didn't follow my friends into a yoga trend. I got my nose pierced but took the stud out two years later because I felt it marked me. (I've had it put back in three times since.) When we had to study different countries in social studies, I would opt for a country that was predominantly white. Greece was a safe bet, France even safer. One girl innocently asked me what kind of food my parents made for dinner, and I roundly told her to go fuck herself. Then, in high school, I was repeatedly called a nigger, because racism doesn't have to be accurate, it just has to be acute. I thought about how much money it might cost for a nose job, something to break down the most obvious ethnic marker I have. All I'd need is some slimming, shattering the cartilage to refit it so I didn't have that Indian bump. Make the tip pointy like a ski jump. (White people love skiing; they're always doing weird shit with snow.) I avoided the sun because, though my skin is a sickly yellow in the winter, it becomes a deep golden brown in the summer.

I pushed against brownness through high school, into university. When I moved to Toronto, the number of brown people I saw in a day tripled, and I resented it, because they knew I was one of them. I didn't want to be in this club.

But then Raisin came out looking like a girl I would ordinarily have considered my enemy. I would have wanted to be her friend because she's cute, objectively. Even I would have seen it at her age, if she were in my class, gliding through life like only a Normal can. And so her life would be (and is) different than mine, because her race is a footnote instead of the title. Unlike me or her father, Raisin isn't being raised Indian; her only real exposure to it comes from my parents, whom she sees twice a week. Her race seems tangential to her existence, hardly something she examines but, rather, something the rest of us have put under a microscope from the minute she started gestating in her mom's insides. My parents felt blessed by her fairness, her light eyes, her distinctly "white" features – typical shadism, the idea that lighter skin is better skin even when it's all brown skin, a frequent topic within brown and black communities but one rarely discussed openly. I was eighteen when she was born and I objectively knew whiteness wasn't better, and yet, weren't we lucky to have a little white girl whose life would never resemble our own?

When Raisin was very small, I rubbed lotion on her belly after a bath and marvelled at how different our skins were: mine a dark yellow, black hair sprouting on my arms and hands, hers like milk and honey. It felt as if I was dirtying her, rubbing my skin against hers when hers was so "good." I wrapped her in a little towel and she looked up at me with blue eyes, the same kind I always wanted for myself.

Jammu is a city of nearly six hundred thousand in the state of Jammu and Kashmir, in the northeast of India.

My mother was raised farther north in Srinagar, in the Kashmir Valley, which is broadly considered a conflict region by most, but Papa's side left the valley in the 1920s. (Mom's parents stayed until the early '90s, when most of the family left after being targeted as both the religious and ethnic minority in their area.) Although Jammu isn't physically in the Kashmir Valley and is therefore not as unstable politically or militarily, the two places are considered inextricably connected; signs across the city boast their connection. Things like J&K government or J&K general store or J&K daycare. Chacha tells us that Jammu and Kashmir has its own set of rules: its own constitution, its own national security regulations, and once its own prime minister. Security crackdowns are so severe here that my phone doesn't work anywhere unless connected to Wi-Fi. Actually, no phones do unless you buy a local SIM card once in the region. No Apple applications work either, another moment where Siri can't do shit for me. Jammu is beautiful, the place I remember most from all our trips to Indian cities. (Mom, however, always reminds me that Srinagar is much more beautiful, all lush trees and floral scents and houseboats. But, considering the region's fluctuations, she has always refused to take us home with her.)

At the Taj Mahal in nearby Agra, people ask Raisin's mother, Ann, if they can hold her daughter. They want to take a photo with her, of her. It gets to be troubling, with strangers trying to pry Raisin out of her mother's arms and Papa chasing people off with aggressive Hindi. I don't totally blame the locals: she is fascinating if you haven't seen a face like that before in nature. She looks white, and I can imagine some people wondering if she isn't a little young for a tourist trip to India. And when they hear her name, an obvious Hindu name, they must marvel at how beautiful she turned out. What fortune that she looks like this instead of like us.

Raisin doesn't seem to notice. She's here for the chai, which is super-sweet and served with cookies from any aunty who can at least understand, "Sugar-tea, please?"

The India of this trip is not the one I remember from fifteen years earlier. Now, I find my preferred type of toilet rather than ones that force you to squat and, inevitably, pee all over yourself. (White people have a lot of flaws, but they did indeed master taking a leisurely forty-three-minute dump while comfortably seated.) Nearly all storefront signs and billboards are entirely in English, the rickshaw drivers know if you're being rude to them, and the men notice that I am an adult woman who makes eye contact and scowls. Signs for "DRUGGIST AND CHEMIST" and "LADY DOCTOR, DR. RANJANA DHAR, TIME: 11 AM TO 12 NOON TUESDAY/FRIDAY" spill into the streets. (What kind of gynecologist only works for one hour, twice a week?) On the back of a car is a sign trumpeting the academic performances of three girls in the public school system, each of whom has a 97 per cent average. The women wear tight jeans and heels and plenty of makeup. I look like a local here, the only obvious sign I'm not being that I rarely colour in my waterline with kajal. (This changes halfway through the trip, when three aunties ask me why I look "so sickly" and start purchasing black eyeliner for me so I can draw thin lines around my eyeballs.)

But most unsettling is how this time I notice my own fairness. I notice that while I might be a person of colour among the diaspora back home, or in any white-majority country, here I am the white person. Kashmiris are notable because there are so few of us left, and because we've taken up a privileged space in India. In Toronto, some Indian cab drivers will ask me where my family is from, and when I tell them, they think they're bonding with me when they talk about how much they hate Muslims. Or, in the case that the driver is Muslim, he'll try to bond with me over the trouble with "the blacks." All of us struggle towards whiteness.

At the wedding venue, a handful of workers make our food and clean our dishes, and all of them are dark-skinned Indians. I can generally pass for whatever race you desire: when I'm in Ecuador, locals speak to me in Spanish; when in Thailand, Thai; I'm mistaken for Greek or Latina or Italian in certain parts of the U.S. But the employees here are undeniably Indian, with undeniable dark skin. When I finish my chai, the same woman who's there all week takes my cup. She prepares us our break-fasts and our hoddles of tea, brings around snacks, does the dishes. She has a saucer-sized nose stud and a flash of white teeth. No one is polite to her, no one says please or thank you, no one except my cousin Sweetu even calls her Aunty, which we were all taught to call someone older than us. When my elders finish their tea and she comes by with a tray, they place their glasses on it without acknowledging her.

It's impossible to ignore that the women who ask for money at the airport are dark-skinned. Or that men whose skin is a few shades darker than mine don't make eye contact, while boys with skin like mine want to talk; they mumble things to me in the streets, they stare at my bare shoulders or stand too close to me in line at the bank. (This happens back home too, but here I notice the difference because here, I foolishly thought we would all look the same.) No one with dark skin works at the bank. No one with dark skin sells us our jewellery or the custom-made Jootas Ann gets, the ones where the toes meet at a point and almost curl, ones we call "Jafar shoes." I don't know what came first, the class differentiations or the shadism, but they are inextricably linked.

When I think about our other trips here, I realize it has always been like this, our entitlement spreading wide out—I just didn't notice until now. On our last trip, my dad let me buy a massive tub of mini-chocolates: a Tupperware filled with Kit Kats and Dairy Milks. When I tore open a wrapper and took a bite, the chocolate disintegrated into some chalky formula, like a dried Tootsie

Roll. We looked closely at the wrappers and saw that they actually said Kit Kit and Dear Milk, a hardly convincing facsimile of something that reminded me of home. Whatever this off-brand chocolate was, it was terrible, but a group of children my age were watching me revolt at what was a pretty significant treat. Even I resent myself in this scene: some chubby, well-fed, fairer-skinned tourist retches at the taste of locally produced chocolate while four other kids watch. I gave them the tub. They took it and ran. I was an asshole.

Or there was the woman who cleaned my Usha Bua's house in Delhi, and how she always wore salwars in neutrals and beige socks that separated the big toe so that she could wear chappals. She made all our meals and seemed to be constantly wiping the floor. She ate her meals standing up in the kitchen while we ate in the dining room at a long wooden table. One afternoon, I was left in the care of Bua's twenty-something son, who barricaded himself in his bedroom. I watched cartoons in the living room while this woman cleaned the house, just like she was always doing. When she passed through the living room one time, though, she paused to watch the show with me for a few minutes. When she caught me looking at her, she took off, but I had just wanted to see if she wanted to sit down with me. Her skin was dark and dewy.

The obsession with fair skin goes beyond what we look like naturally: everyone here wants to look a little bit lighter, particularly the women. Personal ads from parents looking for partners for their children often laud the "wheatish" complexion of their child right next to income and height. Aunties tell me how much I look like my mom, and I know this is a compliment, not just because my mom is beautiful but because she is one of the fairest in the family. Ann tells me that the week before I got here, Bua was rubbing her arm against Ann's, saying she hoped some of the whiteness would come off. Bua does things like this all the time – she's the most concerned about her whiteness, the whiteness of her children. Rohan, her son, is not that fair, but his wife is, so naturally she is a prize. Her daughter Sweetu is even fairer than I am, with slight facial features too, so she is perfect. Bua is not dark, she has never been dark, but I guess the argument stands that she could be lighter. She visited us in Canada once, and circling my face with her chubby hand, asked, "Are you using Fair & Lovely?"

Fair & Lovely is a popular brand of skin-whitener in South Asia, marketed with crummy little ads where a girl gets the guy after she slathers these chemicals on her face and turns into some ghost-like version of her former self. You can buy it for your face or your body, creams to remove "facial discolouration or brown spots," or to lighten all the skin you have, one big body-wide brown spot. There's even a skin-whitening cream marketed for your unacceptably brown labia. Ads show bright women with skin that looks like Cream of Wheat dancing with flowers whizzing around their heads, proof that being fairer will also make you thin, make you beautiful, make men look at you. "Everyone in this stupid country is obsessed with being white," Rohan groans when I tell him about his mother's arm-rubbing. "It's not just her. But she is very invested in it."

When I'm applying my foundation before the wedding – one or two shades lighter than Bua, a little more yellow than brown – she asks me if she can use some. "Sure, I guess," I tell her, "but it's the wrong colour for you."

"But will I look white then?"

I tell her yes, her face will look very white, like that of a clown. She laughs and mumbles something in Kashmiri and pleats her sari faster than my mom and I can unclasp our respective bras.

I have never been this white anywhere in the world. I've never had the most obvious, the most useful kind of privilege as soon as I've walked into a room. This, though, is maybe what it's like to be white. People who look like me in India are assumed to be higher class, in better socio-economic standing, more educated. This is sometimes true, but only because the world here is built to benefit those with light skin and punish those with dark skin, much like the world at home. The caste system is largely defunct in the areas we visit, but that doesn't mean that I and my family aren't still benefiting from decades of racial advantage. The brown people in my family and the others we associate with are almost all wheatish themselves, and have filled my head with Kashmiri superiority, light-skinned dominance, while also suggesting it's something that can't possibly happen in North America. Darker-skinned Indians aren't *bad*, per se, but aren't *we* great? Aren't we smart, and beautiful, and worthy? Isn't that why we're thriving in Canada, in the land of opportunity? The only difference between shadism in India and shadism at home is the level to which my family is served.

Circling the wedding venue throughout the week is a surly young man in his twenties who carries tubs of food back and forth from the venue to the upstairs kitchen. On his shoulders are these cauldrons, big enough to boil a human body, and he slugs them up and down stairs, wordlessly. We never do hear him speak. Or make eye contact. He wears flip-flops while doing manual labour, he smokes cigarettes in the parking lot, he has a smartphone ripping through the back pocket of his very skinny jeans. He's handsome and furious, completely miserable, seemingly unwilling to be there.

I find this irresistible. I follow him around for a few minutes every day, trying to see what I need to do just to get him to look at me. He has a cute butt. Ann agrees, saying she likes his surly yet romantic silence, and posits what her husband or Hamhock might say if we brought this boy home with us. We crack a few jokes about turning him into a respectable man, *My Fair Lady*-ing him, getting him a suit, teaching him English.

This is funny until I remember colonialism.

—

Months after our trip, I visited Raisin and the rest of my family in Calgary. She had just turned six, and still had a few memories of the trip: what she seemed to recall the most was Nice Time, a coconut cookie she was being handed in droves while at the wedding. "Did you have fun?" I asked her.

"Yeah," she said. "But I wouldn't go back for a wedding."

"Why not?" I worried here, because I want her to like it there, or at least to be indifferent about it the way you get to be indifferent about a home when you don't realize you'll miss it one day.

"'Cause you gotta eat the same thing every day! And you hafta wear those outfits, they're so itchy and they never fit! But we can go again, just for fun."

Raisin didn't seem to remember that she thought Indians were all poor – the opulent temples may have convinced her otherwise – or that they all smelled bad – in fact, everything smelled of condensed milk. To her, it was a vacation, and it was a Nice Time, not an identity crisis. She didn't notice skin colour, heritage, or casual racism because she hardly notices her own face. (Though, on this visit, I point to her nose and then to mine and say, "We have the same nose." She loves this and adds, "And the same eyebrows, and when you're grumpy you look like me when I'm grumpy." I'm relieved.)

"Do you think you're brown?" I asked.

"Yeah," she said, "I'm half brown. You're all brown."

"Do you tell your friends you're half brown?" She is passing, always passing for white, and for some reason, I want people to know that she isn't, that we at least tried to have some say in it. I tried to force myself out of brownness at her age, but the older I get, the more I tuck myself into it. My jewellery is almost all gold now: my grandmother's bracelets, her wedding ring, my mom's earrings. When I'm bored, I sometimes draw three dots in a triangle formation on my hand, the same design my mother used to draw in eyeliner on my chin when my Indian dance class had a performance. It's the only place I feel comfortable now.

"Some kids know," she said. "I don't need to tell everyone."

When I talk to Papa about the microaggressions I deal with in my city ("The lady at Starbucks thought my name was Vissagi, and now she keeps writing 'Vissagi' on *aaaaaall myyy cuuuuups*"), he rolls his eyes because he's seen worse. My dad can't pass for white – he is the darkest in the family, with the most Indian nose – so my coffee-cup issue is hardly a problem for him. As a kid, when I went to him complaining about the casual racism I noticed at school, he shrugged. "How do these kids even know you're Indian?" he asked me. "You could be anything."

Which is part of my privilege, though not the whole story, because while you may not be able to pinpoint where I'm from, you know I'm not from *here*. And while Canada purports to be multicultural, Toronto in particular, a place where everyone is holding hands and cops are handing out ice cream cones instead of, say, shooting black men, our inability to talk about race and its complexities actually means our racism is arguably more insidious. We rarely acknowledge it, and when we do, we're punished, as if we're speaking badly of an elderly relative who can't help but make fun of the Irish. The white majority doesn't like being reminded that the cultural landscape is still flawed, still broken, and while my entry into something like Canadian media, for instance, hasn't been an easy ride, it has been made more palatable for other people because I am passable. I'm not white, no, but I'm just close enough that I could be, and just far enough that you know I'm not. I can check off a diversity box for you and I don't make you nervous – at least not on the surface. I'm the whole package!

The racism I noticed as a kid, overt insults said to my face, attempts to demean me and rob me of my humanity, have taken a new form in my adulthood. Now, I'm either ignored or, if I get loud, framed as the stereotypical hotheaded Indian woman screaming and waving a wooden spoon in the streets. People I've worked with – predominantly white women – have told me to "watch my tone" or to be more polite, because a brown woman, any brown woman, can't be too much of anything. I benefit, and yet I suffer in the same breath: bouncers at bars won't reject me out of fear of letting an outfit "get too brown," as has happened to my darker relatives, but

"Yes," she said. "J-a-k-e."

"Who's Jake?" I asked.

"He asked me to marry him," she said. "I think I will." She listed Jake's many accomplishments (can tie his own shoes, can read, can hang from the monkey bars, once fell off the monkey bars and "now knows the pain of biting his own lip"), and I asked if I could come to the wedding. She said okay.

"You should be happy about this," Ann said from the driver's seat.

"Why?" I asked. "They could break up tomorrow."

"Yeah," she said, handing me her phone with a photo of Raisin and her husband-to-be, holding each other and smiling widely. "But Jake's brown."

Papa <papa@gmail.com>, March 14, 2015
You children are getting on my nerves. The problem is very high expectations.

Scaachi <sk@gmail.com>, March 14, 2015
What would you like us to do?

Papa <papa@gmail.com>, March 14, 2015
Treat me like a demigod. Not a full-god, an in-between god. Pay homage to me every time you see me. Do exactly what is in my mind.

Scaachi <sk@gmail.com>, March 14, 2015
What is in your mind?

Papa <papa@gmail.com>, March 14, 2015
I'll think of something.

Aus-piss-ee-ous

———

There are two types of people who insist that Indian weddings are fun. The first are white people, who are frequently well-meaning but stupid and enjoy things vaguely different from themselves by exoticizing them. Do not talk to me about how you love the "colours" of an Indian wedding – the main colours come from blood and shit, not necessarily respectively.

The second type are any people who have never actually been to an Indian wedding in India with Indian people. Or, at least, have never been to the entirety of an Indian wedding, the full five to seven days, the multiple outfits, the familial requirements that forfeit your time and independence. No, these people swoop in for the ceremony and reception, they eat some pakoras and talk about how "cute" it is when little girls have unibrows, maybe they show up early for the henna ceremony and ask for a lower-back tat, and then we never see them again. Indian weddings are a lot of things, but "fun" has never been their purpose.

My family was in Jammu for my cousin Sweetu's wedding. Thanks to an Indian online dating service – Shaadi. com, which means Wedding.com because we as a race are hardly trying – Sweetu's parents were able to arrange her marriage to a nice boy with well-manicured stubble and a good job in America. It's the dream.

If Indian weddings for Indian people are the furthest from "fun," trips to India for Indian people are the furthest from "vacation." When I told my friends about the upcoming trip, everyone purred about what a great time I'd have, told me to take a lot of photos, told me to eat everything. But if you're going to India to see your family, you're not going to relax, you're not going to have a nice time. No, you're going so you can touch the very last of your bloodline, to say hello to the new ones and goodbye to the older ones, since who knows when you'll visit again. You are working.

My parents were in Jammu to give blessings to Sweetu, to send her into her new life accordingly. They arrived with crisp, bank-fresh rupees and red velvet pouches filled with thick gold bangles. My brother and his wife, Ann, were there to show off Raisin, the latest addition to our family, the first grandchild of my father, the eldest son. As for me, a girl and therefore my mother's joy and my father's responsibility, I was there to prove my parents are a success. I was among the first to be born out of India within my extended family, proof positive that my parents moved to a faraway prosperous land for good reason. *Look at me,* I will say merely by showing my beatific face. *I am fair-skinned, of average weight and height, my hair is long and shiny, I am university-educated and respectful of our customs and traditions. I know I don't speak the language, but you can see here on my nose the indent of what was once a nose ring, thus the mark of an authentic but modern Kashmiri girl. The Kouls are thriving in the West. Feel free to signal your approval with a satchel or two of gold.*

After we dropped off our bags at the hotel and after I had a hearty twenty-minute argument with my parents, who neglected to book a separate hotel room for me and were expecting that I would, for fifteen days, sleep sandwiched between my sixty-six-year-old father and sixty-year-old mother (I stopped short of screaming, "I REFUSE TO SLEEP ON THE SAME SURFACE AS YOUR RESPECTIVE GENITALS" before they made up a cot for me on the floor next to their bed), we headed over to the wedding venue, a fifteen-minute auto-rickshaw ride away.

There were already more brown people inside the venue than I had seen in the last five years combined.

Nearly all my father's family was there: his father's last remaining brother; his sister who is actually his aunt (possibly not by blood) but she's younger than him so he calls her his sister; his mother's brother; his actual sister; her son, Rohan, who got married in Delhi a few years earlier with a thousand guests at his reception (I did not go); his daughter, E, the same age as then-five-year-old Raisin; and my dad's cousin, my Vee Masi, my mom's friend who helped arrange my parents' marriage.

If this sounds confusing, that is because it is. Brown people rarely explain how anyone is related to anyone. You're simply told that these people are your family and to treat them as such. My parents do not discuss the fact that one of my "aunts" is actually my dad's aunt, or how my mom's many "sisters" are not her sisters and are sometimes merely childhood friends. It's rude to ask what would otherwise be a very reasonable question: "Hey, Mom, why do you have forty sisters? Was your mother a sea turtle? Is that why she cried so much?" So the question of "how" is maybe less important than the statement of "this": This is your family. You will hear a platitude about how much you look like them even if this is not true. You will smile. You will feel warm. *Behave.*

The venue was a three-floor home with a sprawling lawn for the receptions, a pyre for the ceremony itself, an indoor hall, and multiple rooms for out-of-towners to change and put their children down for naps. In one of the many bedrooms was Sweetu, sitting on a bed with her hair in tiny braids as is customary before a bride's wedding week. (Did I mention Indian weddings last seven days? There are prison sentences that run shorter than Indian weddings.) Sweetu is my actual cousin, her mother being my father's younger sister. This I am pretty sure about, because we look too similar to not share blood. Her hair is long and thick like mine, we have the same nose, same fair and yellowish skin. She's sarcastic and dismissive, somewhat of a hothead until she knows she has to pull it together for the sake of her mother, whose body will literally grow hot when she's angry. Sweetu laughs when everyone gets upset over auspiciousness, a term used nearly constantly at Indian weddings. The accents here also pronounce the word as "aus-piss-ee-ous," fragmented and somehow even more dramatic. The wedding date? Must be *aus-piss-ee-ous*. The pairing itself? Must consult the stars and ensure it is an *aus-piss-ee-ous* union. The placement of napkins, the volume of food circulated, the darkness of the bride's henna? Let us all be sure this is the most *aus-piss-ee-ous* of *aus-piss-ee-ous* days. No one, English-speaking or not, knows what this fucking word means, but it is important that we observe it.

Sweetu is the youngest girl of a youngest girl, the last for her mother to marry off. She is the one who moved to England for a few years to get her education, who wanted to leave India for the U.K. or Canada or the U.S., anywhere that would take her. She's the only one of my cousins — real or otherwise invented — who I can actually see myself in. When I finally got to her, two days of travel and tedious family arguments later, I was reminded of why I'd decided to come to this wedding. "Have you eaten?" she asked me while braiding her little cousin's hair into two thick French braids. "Do you want chai? Milk chai or keheva? Sugar? Let me ask Bhabhi to bring some ch – BHABHI, CHAI CHA?"

I told her she was turning into her mother, my Bua, a woman who barely hits five feet and whose fingers and toes have shrunk from arthritis but who can still pleat a sari faster than any woman I know. She used to call me on the phone and scream, "I LOVE YOU SO MUCH, I AM GOING TO CHOP YOU INTO PIECES SO SMALL, YOU WILL BE A POWDER AND NO ONE WILL FIND YOU." She attacks you with "ARE YOU HUNGRY COME AND EAT SOMETHING" as soon as you walk into a room. She is exhausting and perfect and has the softest skin and she rubs your face with her little warped hands and it is the most love you will ever feel from another human force.

"Well," my cousin replied, "it's not like you aren't turning into her too." I started yelling at her, reaching out to pinch her, until I realized I'd been had.

Sweetu's wedding was an arrangement, but in one of the more generous ways that word can be interpreted. Their parents were involved, and I'm not sure they "dated" in any North American sense. I don't think she and her fiancé spent much time alone before their marriage. But she seemed to like him, and it was clear that she didn't say yes to the first yahoo who tried to whisk her off to America on his green card. Sweetu was twenty-seven at the time, much older than the "ideal" bridal age, and waited until she graduated and was working before she looked for a husband. She had an Instagram account and posted photos of her guy, standing much closer together than I had seen any other girl in our family stand next to a yet unmarried man.

I've never asked her if arrangement was her choice or her parents', but the answer is obvious because this is just how things work here, at least, for our family. So many of my cousins who live in Canada or the U.S. did this too – a modern version of arrangement whereby parents present their daughters and sons with dossiers filled with the opposite sex: "nice boys" (they're always called that, as if being nice is the best thing you can be) with "good jobs" who will take care of their daughters, or elegant, slender-wristed women with wheatish skin who come from "good families" (have you ever heard anything so nebulous?), have money, and will give you attractive, well-behaved, light-skinned babies. Religions have to match. So do class and, inevitably, skin colour.

A few years before this wedding, another cousin of mine who was raised in Alberta was arranged and had her wedding in India. After she married, I asked her why she got arranged instead of finding someone on her own. "I mean, it's not like I'd never met him before the wedding," she said. But even still, her parents monitored and organized the union. Do you trust your parents to make that kind of decision for you? My parents are good at a lot of things – they have made responsible investments with their money, my mom can break an entire lamb down into bite-size pieces on her kitchen island, and my dad scrubs the garage floor biannually, a true testament to his neurosis about garage cleanliness. But I do not want either of them choosing the man I will be stuck with long after their deaths.

The first family marriage I remember not being an arrangement was that of my eldest cousin, Angie. Fifteen years my senior, she was the first of my brother's generation to marry, and to a white boy she met in high school, no less. I was eight, and to me, it was just another wedding. To her, and to the rest of the family, it was an act of revolt – something I learned later, when I found my own white boy to bring home. Angie fought for her choice, her husband forced into the position of a patient object who would have to merely wait his turn for approval. They have a son now, a fourteen-year-old who seems unaware of his role in this now long-forgotten mutiny. (I lived with them for a year when he was seven, and one morning he slipped a piece of paper under my bedroom door that said, "To good will only End of Agurment." If only he knew.)

Papa would love to arrange me. I know because he's asked, and got so angry when I refused that his head filled with all the blood he carries around in his body. Mom probably would have liked it too, but she knew

The wedding had seven different events, each of which required its own outfit—I didn't pack enough, and the ones I brought were, according to my mother, too formal, or not formal enough, or a colour that made me look "sickly, like a—" and here, she pantomimed vomiting. There were ten or twelve outfits stored in my old closet at my parents' house: emerald-green lehengas — two-piece outfits comprising a crop top and a long skirt, embellished with stones and jewels and itchy mesh; salwar kameezes — pants with a long tunic, more silken; and a sari or two — usually reserved for women older than me or, at least, married, because they presumably have the poise to figure out how to piss while precariously hiking up fifteen yards of fabric. (No safety pins means you've levelled up.) Most of the outfits were from my brother's wedding, nearly a decade before. My chest, my hips, my butt, and my thighs had all expanded tremendously since then. Even my neck was thicker. I didn't know that, though, until I tried them all on. Teenage girls of all creeds and colours so often think their bodies are too big, or too small, or too misshapen to be acceptable — we are conditioned to hate ourselves and the ways we're built. So it's surprising when you try to wedge your pancake breasts into a decade-old chiffon top, your arms unable to bend back down, your soft biceps straining the tensile strength of a factory stitching, only to learn that your teenage body was, in fact, *fine*, it was just *fine*. (For all you know, despite your current physical hang-ups, it might still be.)

Outfits are cheaper in India, so my mother wanted to buy another five or six that I would end up wearing only once. I did not want to do this. The preamble to the trip had been an exhausting routine of my mother asking me for my measurements so she could buy me outfits for the wedding, only for her to disagree with me when those measurements were provided.

She called me after I sent my arm circumference and bust size, as requested months before the trip. "No," she said.

"What no?"

"This is not right."

"What isn't?"

"These measurements are not physically possible."

"What the hell does that mean?"

"I've had two children and I'm three times your age. How is it possible that your bust is bigger than mine?"

There are a thousand rational ways to protest this, one of which being that my mother and I are separate human beings who do not share the same body and might therefore be different sizes. Alternatively, I could have argued that because my body has these measurements, it was therefore empirically impossible for them to be impossible. Instead, I felt uncomfortable for weeks before the trip, knowing that this would come up again. My bust: the medical anomaly.

Indian women are naturally curvy, supposedly. This is what people tell me when they look at me sympathetically.

Girls I knew in high school said it to me when they'd see me change for gym class and notice I was all hips and thighs, or when we'd get our swimsuits out for that one misery-making week of swimming that the school forced us to take. ("You know what would be fun," our school's administration likely thought, huffing glue out of an old sock. "What if we make our cruellest eleven-year-olds assess each other in wet spandex for an hour every day for a week in the dead of winter?")

In reality, the bulk of the women I saw there were rail thin, and Indian ideals of beauty continue to be similar to Western ones: fair skin; small, curved waist; doll tits; long, smooth hair; thin nose. Of these qualities, I have the fair skin and naturally straight hair. Jammu is the only place I've ever felt white, and resolutely privileged, and yet my body still feels misplaced. It has never been small enough for any region. It never has the right proportions. My wide shoulders get stuck in shirts, my hips get caught in zippers, my nose juts out of glasses too wide for my small face. My body feels too big for this place. I am too tall, too wide, too much. The girls here, even the ones with a similar shape to mine, barely hit five feet tall. (One afternoon, I put on a form-fitting maxi-dress. My mother told me to think about changing. "It's not that I care," she said. "But you know everyone will talk." She ran her hand along my bloated stomach, filled with chai and fried goods.) I thought my body would make more sense here, that I'd find people with my hips,

my arms, my thighs, my ever-expanding neck. My body
was being wedged into this country at odd angles, shoved
in where it might have never belonged in the first place.

All of this didn't necessarily make me feel bad about
myself until we actually started the torturous process of
shopping for clothes in a country where English was not
a first language and the sales associates were all thirty-
five-year-old men who do not accept that your size is
what you say it is. I was suddenly a teenager again,
embarrassed by and uncomfortable with my body. I had
been dropped into a country that screamed at me even
louder than the place I was born does: *You are not the size
we want you to be.* The process was, predictably, demoral-
izing. In Canada, I could be an 8 or a 10 or a 14, but in
India, I am nothing smaller than an XXL. I tried to not
get too wrapped up in the process – what is, physically
or morally, *wrong* with being of a certain size? Where do
I get off feeling sorry for myself based on an arbitrary
metric that I already know to be bullshit? – but when a
shopkeeper looks at your frame and shakes his head solemnly, it's hard not to take it personally.

The only respite I got for my body in Jammu was from
my hands. When aunties and uncles asked me whose
child I am and I told them my mother's name, their faces
lit up because, of course, I look like her, they could see it
all over me. Then they'd see my hands – my short fingers,
my long nails painted red, the gold rings on two fingers –
and would hold them for a long time in wonder.

Maybe it was foolhardy to think that I'd find my brethren here. Fitting is a luxury rarely given to immigrants, or the children of immigrants. We are stuck in emotional purgatory. Home, somehow, is always the last place you left, and never the place you're in.

Every store we went to during this futile endeavour was complete with at least one outfit that did not go over my head, another one that made it over my head but not my shoulders, and a third that went over my head and down my shoulders but cut off circulation around my breasts, making me look quadra-boobed. I would wear this third one out of the dressing room to show my mother, her disappointment registering so strongly that I think I should bottle it and sell it to people who miss their immigrant mothers and want a lady with great thick grey hair looking at them with deep sadness.

We found three outfits for me over the course of the day. I hated every single one of them.

Attending an Indian wedding means being struck, constantly, violently, by how truly unequal the standards are for men and women, here or abroad. My father and brother weren't required to wear traditional outfits at any point during the wedding. Instead they stuck mostly to sports jackets and polos and cotton tees. They ate and drank freely, they didn't participate in the prayers we chanted around Sweetu's head, and their bodies were rarely up for discussion—a fact I was incensed about mostly because of how alien mine felt to me.

During the Sangeet there was some singing and dancing, provided first by a modern DJ who blasted Indian pop and hip hop—one song bleated "SEX IN THE MORNING" as the hook, making my mother look at me and grimace, and making me want to turn into salt—then later with traditional Kashmiri ghazals sung by live talent.

While the women were downstairs watching everyone dance, and while I was trying to suck my body in so I could fit into this first of many uncomfortable outfits that seemed to creak like old floors every time I took a breath, the men were upstairs getting loaded on cheap whisky and eating fried fish and chicken. I was mostly angry that there were not delicious little pieces of protein circulating for the women, but also that the men were allowed to drink and eat meat on a day reserved for religious activity when both were strictly verboten.

I approached my father on the terrace and he offered me some chicken on the DL.

"Why do you guys get to drink," I asked him, "while the rest of us have to wear dumb outfits and watch crap downstairs and drink Thums Up and Fanta?"

"Because that's the way it always goes."

"That's some patriarchal bullshit," I said between mouthfuls, flecks of fried batter shooting out. "That's hypocritical and I hate it on a feminist level."

"As you should."

"But you're participating in it."

"Ah, well," he said, drinking the rest of his boozy syrup. "What're y'gonna do."

Arguing over traditions that have been in place forever is so consuming that neither of us even began to try. But this version of my father, a man who was lazily dropping fried fillets into his mouth, was hard to square with the same man who demanded I get an education, pay my own bills, and take care of myself before considering even communicating with a human man. Even though he was born in the 1950s, I think he was doing his best and most convincing impression of a passive feminist. And yet, it's likely easier for men in India to not get too tied up with these little inequities. I hate the narrative that Indian people are backwards, that they are more barbarian, more animalistic. That's not what it is, but some of them do have priorities that do not include who gets to eat at the fish-fry.

I don't know how long customs like this – outdated ones, because, again, I want fried chicken – can be sustained. The younger girls who were dancing downstairs with the bride, all younger than thirty, were constantly on their phones and their English was flawless and they all wanted to move to America. I can't imagine any of them being happy with the men in their families getting loaded on another floor while they're resigned to flat soda in paper cups.

My cousin Rohan, the bride's brother, patted me on the shoulder and muttered, "Do you want me to see if I can bring you a drink?" Rohan was halfway between my age and my parents' age, obedient to his family, but very aware of how dumb I found all this.

"Always, and forever, as long as I am alive," I said.

"Give me a few minutes." Maybe some people are trying, albeit quietly, to change things.

When I returned downstairs, Sweetu had endured yet another outfit change, and the mehndi that was painstakingly applied to her arms and legs and feet and hands had dried and was flaking off. The man singing to her and the rest of the family was a young, classically handsome Kashmiri, with tanned skin, brilliant teeth, and thick, curly dark hair that had been shaped into an Elvis mullet. I liked him. His face was charming and funny and sweet. He was wearing a dress and had churia around his wrists, thick anklets that jingled, and little bells strapped around his legs from the knees down. Slowly, the men oozed their way back downstairs, gabbing loudly, largely ignoring the performance. Our man in the dress hopped around the venue singing to different family members, calling out the bride's uncles (my father and Chacha joined him near the stage to dance awkwardly with him) and then her parents. He pulled my mother up onstage with him, singing to her and getting her to dance. When the dancer asked her, in singsong Kashmiri, "Who is your hero?" my father marched over to collect her in mock rage and said, "Me, goddamn it," pointing aggressively at his chest with one hand and dragging my laughing mother away with the other.

Sweetu came up to me and wrapped her arms around my shoulders and pulled me in for a hug, smelling like drying henna and old sweat from the three straight hours of dancing. "Are you having fun?" she asked in her gentle Indian-British accent.

"I am, but explain the man in the dress to me. Is it supposed to be funny that he's in a dress?"

"Yes. He's acting like a woman."

"But why does he have to be in a dress?"

"Because what fun is it to watch someone dance when they're not in a dress?"

"But, why is it funny?" This show was such an obvious play on queerness, on transphobia, but also the showcasing of women. Women as items, women as entertainment, women as commodities. Men as women as sexualized jokes.

"Look," she said, exasperated. "You are in a very hypocritical country. Women cannot dance in front of men, but a man in a dress, he can dance in front of men. It's all a big joke. On women." She laughed and pinched my cheeks when she said this, a sentence that should have made me angry, and should have hurt, but somehow made me laugh back.

What isn't a joke on women, either here or back at home? Sweetu is empowered, she always has been, at least from my vantage. But so much about this wedding meant tolerating customs or traditions or experiences that barely treat women as human. When Sweetu wasn't being reduced to merely existing as a bride, as a piece of meat to be handled and prodded, to have decorative contraptions stuck into her skull, her interests were otherwise unexpressed. She rarely complained, hardly asked for anything, and maybe that's because Indian girls grow up going to weddings and we watch the procedure and we know our roles: be demure, don't complain, cry but don't scream, get tea for anyone older than you, and calmly meet expectations.

Sometimes Hamhock takes my left hand and holds it to his face and asks me when I'll come around to getting married, when I'll let him propose. I always say later, not now, no real date in mind, not because I want to torture him (though that is fun), but because I know what it would mean. All Hamhock wants is a big one-day bash for everyone we love, for his friends to be able to drink freely, eat whatever they want, and for us to get a toaster in the process. He is a sweet, precious moron who doesn't know any better because he was never eight years old at his eldest cousin's wedding, watching her body get doused in milk and rose petals and later yogurt to cleanse her before the wedding. He didn't watch a man dance in women's clothing because a woman was not allowed to. He would get to eat fried chicken and drink shit-shelf whisky with the men while one of my aunties gave me a lecture on being a "good" wife. He would be given the benefit of the doubt; I would have to be educated.

My parents would like us to get married (we're living in sin and that's far worse than an age gap or racial difference),

SCAACHI KOUL

and they've claimed they'd be fine with a courthouse wedding, a run to Vegas. They are liars. In the fifth grade, I got my hair chopped off in an ill-advised pixie cut, some two feet of dark black hair sheared off me like a sheep. Mom gathered it all and stuffed it into a heavy-duty Ziploc bag. "What are you doing?" I asked her as she tucked the bag into her purse. "When you're older," she said, "you're going to get married, and this we can use for hair extensions on your wedding day." She put the hair in the deep-freezer in the garage and it's still there; sometimes when I root around for Pizza Pockets I will instead pull out a bag filled with my DNA. My mother would like a wedding, please, and it is not optional.

Mom used to tell me that white people don't understand us, would never understand us, even when they are well-meaning and patient. At the time, this was her argument for why so few of us married anyone besides a fellow Kashmiri, or at least a fellow Hindu. I thought she was being reductive and unforgiving, but she might have known something I didn't: how do I explain to Hamhock, who feels only love and little obligation, that my life comes with an excess of the latter? You marry into this, whether you like it or not. The wedding is merely the first step in a lifelong commitment to rituals and customs that barely make sense even to the elders who propagate them.

And after all that, Rohan never did bring me that drink.

—

On the day of the ceremony—day *five*, by the way; it's a full *five days* before we get around to the actual ceremony—I was wearing a distressed long-sleeved Blue Jays shirt. I wore it because I refused to put on my six-pound lehenga, itchy and clunky with its mesh and beading, more than two minutes before I absolutely had to.

"Do you have a *nice* T-shirt you can wear instead?" Mom asked me.

"What's wrong with this one?"

"It looks like it came from . . . from . . ." My mother struggled to finish her sentence. She does this sometimes, when she's speaking in English and she can't find the words she wants, usually when she is going to insult me.

"From?"

"Some sort of . . . garbage pile."

I'm not so much insulted that she has, for what is maybe the fourth time on this trip, asked me to change my outfit, but rather that this is her weakest insult yet. We had only been here a few days. It was too early to slip.

Although the ceremony didn't technically start until 6 p.m., Standard Brown Time, meaning it would actually start at seven (it ended up starting at eight), we dutifully headed over to the venue at ten in the morning. When we got there, Sweetu was the most sage and collected bride I've ever seen, largely because I think that by the time you reach day five, you realize how little is in your control. You do not pick your outfits, your meals, the times of day you get to take a shit, or whether there will be some creepy-crawly younger cousin sleeping in the bed next to you. It doesn't matter what you want because this day isn't for you, it's for your mother, you idiot, so just look nice and say "Namaskar" when someone walks in. Which is exactly what Sweetu did when we entered.

After a few hours of our routine (chai, roti, butter, chai), the process of preparing Sweetu's hair began. Flanked by pillows, one of her aunties sat beside her, with her other female cousins and me sitting by her side. Aunty slathered her hair in coconut oil, root to tip, while other aunties wailed Indian songs that I couldn't understand.

Once Sweetu's hair was slicked down, Aunty painstakingly parted it down the centre, something that should have taken two, maybe three seconds, but because they wouldn't use a comb ("They're not allowed," my mother said, which she used as a justification for every harebrained act throughout the week) and because all the aunties wanted to be involved, no one could agree on whether it was parted straight. Over and over, Sweetu's hair was brushed back by fingers, parted by long nails, until they eventually agreed that yes, sure, this is acceptable. Aunty braided each side of Sweetu's hair in a long, rope-like braid, weaving into it red threads with golden tassels at their ends. Then, wrapped over her braids, was a thick gold ribbon. They tied a beaded headdress around her forehead, and this was when I saw Sweetu start to sweat. Aunties had been pulling and prodding her hair for forty-five minutes by then. The headdress was the least of her concerns, though, because on top of it went a white strip of fabric, tugged tight, stretched over her skin and oily hair. I patted Sweetu on the knee. She whimpered.

They added a golden hat made of thin, shimmery synthetic fabric. Then a white sheet with gold stars and stitching. Then another headdress. Finally, to fasten it all, the aunties barked at me to retrieve some pins from a grey shopping bag I'd been handed earlier in the day. I am not a psychopath, so I assumed they meant bobby pins, but they are safety pins. Three grown women held Sweetu's head and started safety-pinning the entire contraption into her hair, stabbing her skull with little pricks. Finally, she broke, bawling, big heavy tears that didn't even run down her face but fell straight out of her eyes onto the ground. In response, the aunties hooted and hollered and laughed, maybe because this was all a part of the process, maybe because they thought she was crying because of the beauty of marriage or because Indian brides are just supposed to be sad on their wedding day. To them, she was a girl becoming a woman, despite being in her late twenties. Maybe that was the reason for the tears. But I still think Sweetu was crying because they were poking safety pins into her skull.

It was hardly the first time Sweetu's family had seemingly derived joy from her clear displays of pain. Earlier in the week, she'd been subjected to one of the most painful (and yet mandatory) moments, with the insertion of the dejhoor, a gold chain with a swinging gold pendant hanging off it shaped like an engraved football – a piece of jewellery that signals a married woman the way a ring often does. The dejhoor is threaded through a piercing in the cartilage of each ear, right in the centre, a place typically reserved for little studs or hoops, not chain-link that must be pulled through an incision in a part of the body that does not flex. For now, they used red thread instead of the chain, with the ornament attached, but it's still massively painful to have thick gold amulets hanging from the sides of your head. Sweetu sat in front of the fire and wept, begging them to be gentle.

Her to-be, meanwhile, had to do none of that. At my brother's wedding a near decade earlier, he was forced to eat a salty traditional pudding that tastes like cold vomit, hug hundreds of near-strangers, and pray for an hour in front of a hot fire in the dog days of summer, but nothing was threaded through man-made holes in his body. I resented that no holes were being punched into the groom's head for the occasion. When the dejhoor ceremony was over, Sweetu found me on the roof of the wedding venue and half-collapsed on my shoulder in exaggerated exhaustion.

"This is too much," she said. "It never ends." Her face was drained of colour and she gave me a weak smile, twirling my hair around her finger.

"Well," I said, "the good news is that one day we'll all be dead and none of this will matter." Sweetu let out a heavy, desperate laugh, pinched my cheek just hard enough to hurt, and floated off to her next obligation.

An hour after the time the wedding was supposed to start, my cousin Birdie and I walked down to the front entrance with some of Sweetu's other relatives to receive the groom. He was late. We waited at the end of a long carpeted runway for him to show up, bearing thalis filled with marigold petals. Others, including my brother and a very tired and weepy Raisin, held garlands to offer. We waited another hour.

The groom eventually arrived wearing crushed burgundy velvet from head to toe, draped in fresh flowers and money. We began the procession towards the pyre, Birdie and I tossing marigold petals at him as he walked. We moved towards a teeming crowd standing at the door, more aunties and uncles bearing garlands, and when they placed them around the groom's neck, we had to stop for photos and for the video team. People ended up doing this repeatedly just to get the photo right, staging themselves just so, as if anyone gives a shit what *you* looked like at someone else's wedding.

Once he was in, Birdie and I went back upstairs to get Sweetu. She was draped in an endless loop of red fabric with gold stitching, abstract flowers and leaves and vines, the border of her sari thick with embroidery. She wore at least seven gold necklaces, little pearls and rubies and the black stones that Indian women wear once they get married. Her lips were painted candy-apple red, her eyes lined with thin black liner, her cheeks had been pinched, a bindi placed dead centre on her forehead, just below a dangling piece of jewellery that hung from her part, underneath the headdress. I told her she looked beautiful, because she did.

"Really?" she asked, as if it would be possible for her to be anything but. "I feel strange."

"No, you look perfect. Really." I detangled one dejhoor from her other necklaces and inadvertently pulled her ear. She yelped. I took eight big steps backwards.

And now, soon, filled with blessings, the bride and groom would get married, and we would all watch, and it would be beautiful.

This is not what happened. This is not what happened because this was an Indian wedding and Indian people have planned it so nothing goes the way you want it to go because no one seems to agree on what is supposed to happen. While we were walking Sweetu to the pyre, I was trying to figure out how the thousand or so guests would be able to watch the ceremony—the space was hardly big enough for the immediate family during the prayer ceremonies. I asked Birdie, who laughed right in my stupid face because it's in moments like these that I reveal myself to be an outsider. "First of all, the ceremony lasts all night," she said. Define *all night*.

"All night. It will go on until tomorrow morning. And no one is going to watch the ceremony. Everyone will go eat and relax and sit outside and when they get tired, they'll go home." It was 9 p.m. This ceremony was going to last another nine hours.

I spent the night drifting around the venue listlessly. By eleven, I had changed into a sweater and jeans, one of my mother's wool shawls wrapped around my shoulders. I ate fried eggplant and little slices of lotus root swimming in yogurt marinade. I drowned myself in tea and cookies. Hours of the night went by in which I didn't see anyone I recognized. At four in the morning, I remembered that it was Hamhock's birthday, but I had no Wi-Fi, and no active SIM card, and no way to tell him that I was sorry I took this weird trip without him. I held my useless phone, wrapped myself in my mother's shawl, and cried in the fetal position in the now-empty reception hall. *Why is it so cold here?* I thought. *It's India. The only thing India is required to be is hot.*

Papa found me after a few hours and woke me up to come outside so we could walk Sweetu to her new life. Customarily, as they have for hundreds of years, new brides leave their weddings to go live with the family of their husband – my mother did the same when she got married. For a few years, she was living with my dad's parents, and later, when his father died, with my Chacha. Sweetu was off to do the same, if only temporarily, before she and her husband moved to North America. We were saying goodbye.

At six, we began the procession back out from where we'd brought the groom in. I had been deeply grumpy most of this trip, sullen like a teenager unwilling to

participate in a school play, irritable about limited
Facebook time and even less time alone, preferably in a
room without my parents. But in that moment I had
lost my instinct for negativity, for wanting to be anywhere else. It was the one moment in our entire trip
when I didn't hear a constant cacophony: children
screaming in the streets, motorized scooters driving
directly into each other, the endless din of Indian
women talking, talking, talking. There was no moon,
no sun, just the reddish dusty swirls of unpaved road
getting swept up in the wind and a navy sky behind
pink and orange drapery.

As Sweetu made her way through the crowd, no one
talked. The only sound filling the frigid air was sniffing
and tissues being stuffed into faces. Sweetu got to me,
her eyes glazing over and makeup melting down her
face. She hugged me around my neck and I didn't know
what to do, I rarely know what to do with brides, I never
know what to do with a crying bride. "It's okay," I told
her. "I'll be on the other side of the hemisphere too."

Sweetu took a step towards the car, then swivelled
back to her mother, standing behind her. They held
each other for what felt like a world-stopping lifetime.
It made me want to rip my heart out and hand it to
them because mine will never be used as much as these
two were using theirs.

She waved goodbye from the car as she and her new
husband departed for his parents' home. Bua watched the

car drive off, her little warped hands over her heart. She turned away and crumpled, her whole body shaking and hiccupping with sobs. She covered her face and cried as we all walked back to the venue for tea, of course, more tea.

But I don't know what we were all fucking crying about because Sweetu returned from her husband's home a laughable seven hours later.

Her in-laws had removed her headdress and washed the oil out of her hair. She'd been unwrapped and re-wrapped in another bright-red sari, her hair pinned up into an elegant bun. She hadn't slept, and I'm not entirely sure she'd eaten anything since the evening before, but she looked transformed. Sweetu was an adult now, a real woman in a woman's clothes and hair and makeup and a legitimate dejhoor, the strings replaced with gold chains, hanging off her ears. These are the signs, I guess.

Arranged marriages still make me uneasy, and their implication — that the woman is being sold into middle-class slavery — is nefarious. Certainly that's true for plenty of women, and not just in India, but it was nice to see Sweetu and her new husband smile and swap whispered jokes and touch in fleeting moments that were more intimate than the interactions of some of the white couples I know. They gazed at each other in comfortable silence while the chaos of a brown wedding continued to dart around them. For them, it works, it's working, it's the most anyone can ask of a marriage. And good, because that wedding was endless, so it had better work out.

—

Descriptions of India are, so frequently, splashed with bright colours and charming poverty. When white people set movies or music videos in India, they often depict the spring festival of Holi, with coffee-skinned people throwing powder at each other while wearing white. In some regions, this does happen, but there's something odd about other people using depictions of this holiday with no thought to when it actually takes place. Imagine if brown people kept making movies in which people were celebrating President's Day for no discernible reason.

People allow India to exist only in two versions. In the first, everything is too beautiful to be encapsulated, women are swarthy and hippy, shoeless boys play soccer in dirt roads, elephants roam the streets, and temples are merely there for your enjoyment. In the second, India is a country lurching forward awkwardly, suffering a rape epidemic, incapable of a feminist movement or proper health care, a place where people shit and piss in the streets, where the caste system has ruined entire generations, where poverty is so rampant and depressing that you'll hardly make it out with your soul intact, where your IT centre is based, a place just close enough to Pakistan or Iraq or Afghanistan to be scary, but stable enough to be fun and exotic. Because, boy, isn't the food good, and aren't the landmarks something, and hasn't everyone there figured out a kind of profound meditative inner peace that we should all learn from? Like all things, the truth lies somewhere in the middle. A place, any place, can be beautiful and perfect and damaged and dangerous at the same time.

After our final wedding meal – another lunch, another tub of dum aloo and collard greens pressure-cooked to death – we had to go. Sweetu was to leave the country in a few days too, to move to Appalachia with her husband. That's where she will start to lose and forget things. That's where the pieces of the family get fragmented again. That's where her children will lose this language eventually, where their children will not even be sure where their grandmother was from. That's where India becomes a place she was from and not a place she lives. That's where her roots get pulled out. I didn't tell her this, because this would be a stupid thing to hear from someone who never lived here in the first place. Instead, I hugged her, and she smelled good, like every woman in India seemed to smell: sandalwood, fragrant hair, Nivea.

"So, when will I see you next?" she asked, her wedding bangles jangling ceaselessly. "The next marriage?"

"Sweetu, you'll be eight hours from me. If it takes us a decade to see each other, something is wrong."

She hugged me again, pinching my cheeks because I am forever younger than her. I walked away as Raisin ran in front of me, trying to rip off the last Indian outfit she was required to wear on this trip.

So much of immigration is about loss. First you lose bodies: people who die, people whose deaths you missed.

Then you lose history: no one speaks the language any-more, and successive generations grow more and more westernized. Then you lose memory: throughout this trip, I tried to place people, where I had met them, how I knew them. I can't remember anything anymore. Raisin doesn't even try. I never miss any of these losses until I'm reminded they exist, until weddings or funerals or births or other milestones of a life cycle. I don't like the obliga-tion of a wedding, but I did like the look on my mom's face when she watched Sweetu float to the car to be carted off to her father-in-law's home. I liked how she rested her chin on her hands and blinked thick tears, good ones, the kind you want your mother to one day cry for you. I liked that she got some closure, that she got to send someone off the way she was sent off. Mom com-plains about having to clean rooms in my childhood home that have long been empty, but when anyone sug-gests downsizing, she demurs. "I don't want to sell this house until you get married. This is your house. I have to send you off from this house." I don't want to wear the old hair that my mother has stored in her deep-freezer, but I like that she considered it.

One day, Hamhock and I will have to do this, less for us than for my parents, and my Bua, and Chacha, and Chachi, and Masi, and Fufaji, and all the fragmented parts of our family who may not attend but will some-how have a hand in threading a chain through my ear or force-feeding me little fried chilies. Hamhock will do it because he loves me and I will do it because I love him, but above all, I will do it to give my family an ending, a promise that I remember parts of our history that I can't possibly know. I will do it because it tells them that I'm okay, that the circle my parents drew is closed, and now I can start a new one. There's so much of it that I don't want—there will not be gender-specific sobriety, *thank you*—but when else will I get all these people into a room, wearing chiffon and eating with their hands, to wish me off into a good life? When else might I see them again?

Raisin often tells me I'm not an adult because I'm not married, suggesting that it might be time for me and Hamhock to get on with it. I laugh at her, but I want the same for her, too, eventually. I don't care who she marries—frankly, I don't even care if it's a legal union. I just want to rub coconut oil in her hair and tell her that she is in my bones, no matter where she ends up. I, too, will cheer and laugh when they press safety pins into her head, or cover her in milk infused with purple flowers, or when she complains about the impressive weight of an intrusive outfit. A little torture, a few tears, some gold around her wrist and neck, the gentle application of bindis along her eyebrows—after all these years we've spent away from each other, it is the very least she can give me.

Mute

———

My first computer was a forty-seven-pound Dell desktop, the monitor the size of a filing cabinet and a tower tall enough to – theoretically – prop your leg up on when masturbating. My parents got it for me when I was twelve, the year my brother moved out of the house for law school and the year I started seventh grade. It wasn't the first computer we had – my dad had his work laptop, the one with the little red nipple in the middle of the keyboard that you had to tweak to get the mouse to move. Then there was the desktop computer years before the laptop and the Dell, a clunky white beast with a fan that whirred so loudly my mother could hear it from the floor below me. All I did on it was fuss with Microsoft Paint, or try to play "King's Quest VI," despite barely being able to read, or type out letters in Wingdings to send to aliens – you know, the specific breed of alien who speaks exclusively in MS Wingdings.

But this computer, this one had internet. Real internet, the internet that didn't fuck up the phone. Internet that my parents didn't completely understand and, therefore, internet that led to true freedom. It was 2003, and this was the quiet rebellion I could hold. My parents told me I wasn't allowed to use any instant messengers or join social networks, but name one preteen who obeys their parents, even if they're just trying to keep their child from being abducted. ("FUCK YOU, MOM, THIS GUY SAYS HE'S EIGHTEEN AND HE WANTS TO MEET UP WITH ME IN HIS VAN AND YOU CAN'T STOP ME FROM FALLING IN LOVE!!!") My twenty-five-year-old cousin, Neeta, set up my webcam and Hotmail account and MSN Messenger. She assured my parents I could never contact a stranger, winking at me behind their backs.

I spent every free moment I had online, ignoring the homework the computer was intended for and instead watching clips of Jon Stewart on *The Daily Show* or heading over to MiniClip.com to play a video of Hillary Clinton's head on an animated stripper's body. I chatted online with my friends from school and made new ones, getting into heated arguments on message boards about things that didn't really matter but felt like they were the *only* things that mattered. Boys paid attention to me and girls were threatened by me. The internet rewarded all the parts of my personality that the tangible world didn't: sarcasm, cynicism, and a refusal to enjoy almost anything. At that time, our corner of the internet gave you full control of your image, so I edited my profile photos to make my skin look its best and snapped pictures from flattering angles only. (Imagine if a bird snatched the camera from your hand and took a photo just as it flew directly over your cleavage.) I got to be smart, too, discussing newspaper articles I had read (if you say things incredulously like "The real estate market *alone*," just about anyone will take you seriously) and chatted about sports I pretended to like — when a guy sent me a message asking me about my favourite football team, all I needed were quick fingers and reliable Google sources to pretend I knew what a down was. My MSN name, meanwhile, was GoOd GiRlS aRe BaD gIrLs ThAt HaVeN't BeEn CaUgHt.

Does anyone remember Nexopia? I suspect not, but it was popular in western Canada from the early to mid aughts. It was like a Canadian knock-off of MySpace, but, like all Canadian knock-offs, it was much worse. You could customize your account with thumbnail-sized GIFs, and if you paid around ten bucks a month, you could further personalize your profile with colours and fonts of your choosing. It was, predictably, hell. If you were popular at school, you were popular on Nexopia.

If you weren't, the site largely just recreated the same social structures you had in the physical world: you, quietly lurking around Melanie and her tattoo (*oh my god, I can't believe she has a tattoo at fourteen, she is cool and I am a skunk ape*) while convening with your friends in private channels far away from everyone else.

For plenty of girls using the site, it was our first foray into what we would later call online harassment. It would be years, maybe a decade, before any of us would know what to call it. When we were thirteen, it was simple: if you were stupid enough to take a photo of yourself and post it online showing an inch too much clavicle, or if you dared develop early and your tits naturally hovered right below your chin, you would get weird messages from men. They'd ask you for something, or threaten you if you were too bold and they didn't like it. That was *your* fault. It was *your* fault if they asked to meet up, then became vaguely threatening when you said no. Sometimes this wasn't so vague, like when they threatened to find your address if you refused to send n00dz. You owed them something, whatever they decided it was that afternoon. We all assumed this was normal. We were barely teenagers, and when older men sent us messages that were creepy at best and threatening at worst, it was expected. What was valued above all, despite how some of us used the site to be smart and clever, was our femaleness. We were girls, so it dragged attention towards us and then tried to make us feel bad for it.

Schoolyard squabbles became hyperaggressive feats of manipulation on Nexopia. Girls would catfish each other, pretending to be a cute boy from a nearby school. (No need to use your real name on Nexopia.) Boys would receive a PG-13 text from a girl and share it with each other, creating little vortexes of mini-scandals. Worse, perhaps, was Nexopia's rating system, in which your profile pictures were automatically fed into a slideshow where anyone on the site could rate your hotness on a scale of 1 to 10. Just a few thousand thirteen- to eighteen-year-olds leaving each other messages about how fat and/or fuckable you were.

This is glorious when you're a teenager and the world is only as big as you allow it to be. Even the internet didn't feel like the all-encompassing thing it actually is; at the time, going viral wasn't a possibility, so the shared videos of backyard fights were only for us. When I wrote a mean blog post about a girl in my grade eight math class, she found it, and her friends found it, and they sent me a few irritated Nexopia messages, but it blew over in an hour. Any criticism you got felt self-contained. Any compliments filled you with only a temporary glow. You still had to leave the house and go back to school; your mom would make you.

Then many of us made the internet our job. We got tiny computers that fit in our pockets so we could check them at bars, at restaurants, while we were languishing pants-down on unkempt toilets in order to avoid small talk at an ill-conceived party. And we found each other on it, again, and took all the lessons we had learned from our small, intense, intimate online communities and tried to apply them to this bigger, bolder, unwieldy global internet.

I use Twitter – a lot. Possibly more than I should. I use it for work, I use it to play, I turn it on and say, "Mmm, sorry, this is important," and act like it's an urgent email when I run into a girl who three years ago called me "pretty for my size." Twitter is how I first met Hamhock – he followed me a year before we would meet in person. I liked his profile picture, and when I asked others about him, I was told he was married with twin daughters. This proved untrue, but will make for interesting hindsight should I ever hear about his second family located somewhere in the Pacific Northwest.

Most people use Twitter to drain their brains of the things you can't say in public, the minor irritations of existence, passive aggression so sharp that if you acted it out at your office you would immediately be fired. But me, I am a loudmouth, all the time, anytime, virtually and in person. (For the last six years, I've been in a heated argument with my former editor and current nemesis, Jordan, over whether it's spelled *woah* or *whoa*, with me championing the former. He might be right, but frankly, I'm in too deep and I would sooner die than let him think that *whoa* doesn't look fucking ludicrous.) So Twitter is a place for me to go and yell into the ether, and for the ether to come into focus as other people, and for those other people to scream back in my face. It is nothing if not even-handed.

It's hard to predict what will attract the internet's ire. Men – and in my experience they are almost always men, white men, straight white men, middle-class straight white men, with "anti-Marxist" and "anti-feminist" in their Twitter bios – cannot be relied upon for consistent outrage. Say what you will about online feminist activism: we are very predictable. You know we're here to yell about equal wages, abortion access, the ability to go outside without being catcalled. But when you're contacted by a guy whose Twitter bio says "Sacred cows make the tastiest steak tartare," well, that's impossible to track.

I was yelled at for making jokes about the very stupid white woman I once saw wearing a row of five (FIVE) bindis on her forehead in public at seven in the morning. That one yielded a week of people accusing me of reverse racism. I was yelled at by Men's Rights Activists for going on television and arguing that a 50/50 gender-split in the Senate would be a good thing. There's one guy – and I honestly wish I were making up this name because it is too perfect to be true and he's likely deleted his account by now so who will ever believe me – whose Twitter name is Brian Jerkey. Jerkey likes to send me tweets in which he tells me I'm dumb, or, in one eloquent rush, repeated missives of "BOOOOOOOOO." We are married now.

One of the longest online spats I got dragged into
lasted four days, winding down only when I started to
reply to angry tweets with passages from *Good Will
Hunting*. I dug up the script online and read through the
worst, hackiest quotes possible, mostly because I was
tired of fighting nonsense with logic rather than, well,
unrelated nonsense.

"The slightest hint of actual research would blow your
entire house of cards down," said a man whose online
pseudonym was A Jackass In Rags. He was, of course,
upset with nearly my entire gender, using me as an easy
representative of 51 per cent of the population.

"It's not your fault," I answered, hoping he would
eventually break down crying in my arms, me the sage
teacher, him the damaged student.

"I know it's hard through the 'poor me' victim haze,"
Jackass continued, "but we're trying to get you [to] a
coherent stream of thought."

"I bet you can't even tell me what it smells like in the
Sistine Chapel."

"What can one really expect from a gender bigot?"

"STOP JERKING OFF IN MY MOTHER'S ROOM!!!"

This went on well into the night, and it was hours
before any of my critics realized that these were movie
quotes and that I did not actually want to know what
they thought about "them apples." I went to bed at two
in the morning, feeling moderately victorious. The next
morning, Hamhock shook me awake, his iPhone in his

hand, my tweets flickering on his screen. "What," he asked, "were you *doing* last night?"

I sometimes try to understand how people formed their identities in eras before the internet existed. What did teenagers do to carve out a sense of self in the world? So often, the people screaming at me online seem to derive their selfhood from being internet aggressors, and the more time I spend on any given online platform, the more my identity is marked by defending myself. I know *Good Will Hunting* quotes by heart now. Obscure ones. Ones like, "I swallowed a bug!" You can't come back from that.

For those of us who are not in a position of power – us women, us non-white people, those who are trans or queer or whatever it is that identifies us as inherently different – the internet means the world has a place to scream at us. The arguments range from the casually rude – people who want me to lose my job, or who accuse my father of leaving me and my mother, which would explain all my issues with authority – to comments deeply disturbing, ones that even my greatest enemies wouldn't verbalize to my face. Not just offensive comments on my body or my skin colour but rape threats, death threats. Accusations that I'm a terrorist. Encouragements for suicide. I answered a lot of them, because your brain fills with toxins so fast when someone threatens you with forced fellatio that you need to exercise that energy, somehow, even if the way to do it means making another dick joke.

People ask me how I handle this. "Doesn't it wear you down?" one friend asked after I showed her my Twitter mentions, filling with men calling me a cunt or a whore or threatening to detach my limbs and toss me into a dumpster. It doesn't – or, rather, it didn't – for the same reason that you're not supposed to be afraid of non-poisonous spiders. They're more afraid of you, and they're only displaying a panic response when their legs freak out and they start running around your walls in circles. Why waste my finite fear and rage on what is, ultimately, something my cat can trap and eat out of her little pink paws?

When I've interacted with these men – and again, they are, by and large, all men, very angry men – they all betray some information about their trauma. After a year or so of mocking them, I started asking, directly, what happened to them. Sometimes I'd just apologize preemptively for what was so obviously a personal destruction they were trying to soothe. Their wives had left them for another man, maybe a friend, sometimes a relative. Their children were taken too, suddenly, and they blamed the women in their lives for not taking better care of their offspring or for refusing to let them have shared custody. They lost their job to a woman or a non-white person, someone they deemed unqualified, someone who didn't need the money like they did. They went to war and returned with PTSD and mental health issues, and neither the government nor their personal support networks took care of them the way we all hope and like to think the country takes care of its veterans. Their moms died. Their moms abandoned them. Their uncles molested them. They were raped in jail. They were raped by women. Their fathers beat them and beat their mothers and told them, "This is how the world works." One man sent me thousands and thousands of words in an email, explaining how his mother killed herself recently, and how it was my fault. I told him I was sorry for what happened. He immediately replied, apologizing for his letter.

Or they just hate women. They hate brown women who do not fit a stereotype they're comfortable with, but frankly, they hate those women too. Sometimes there isn't logic. Sometimes they just think I'm a cunt.

It is taxing to consider the circumstances that can take an unmarked human canvas and make it rage-filled and petty and lost. It's not fun to have sympathy for the people who are trying to hurt you. But their actions can sometimes make sense: what's easier than trying to get better is trying to break something else down. It gives credence to your power, a power you might not always feel. It tells the world that you have value, since the person who was supposed to tell you that you had value left in the middle of the night. Or didn't give you medication when you needed it. Or touched you where they shouldn't have. These men who harass women online were all owed something very simple at one time—respect, love, affection, the basic decency of living upwards and not curling inwards, a humane education—and someone, along the line, failed them.

It's so obvious that when these men yell at me and try to get me fired and threaten to have me killed they're angry at both the entire world and specific people, people I don't even know, people I have never met, people who did far worse things than my mere existence could ever do. It doesn't make me feel better about it, it doesn't make me like it, but it does give me an answer.

I probably should have been afraid sooner. People told me to be afraid, to reset my passwords weekly, to be wary of my address or my parents' address getting posted online. But my fear does not come from an endless trove; I would much rather direct it to things that actually scare me. I'm afraid of my parents dying and having to settle their estate. I'm afraid of Raisin growing up to be a jerk and then reconciling my unconditional love with wanting to punch her in the mouth. I'm afraid of waking up to discover Hamhock has had a stroke in his sleep despite him being significantly healthier than me. Fear always reaches a breaking point and turns into anxiety or rage, and I don't have enough storage space for more fear in my life. Namely when it involves people I've never even met.

It took me six years of using Twitter before I snapped. I was brave, unthinkingly, for six years, fielding the odd crude comment or harassment campaign. But the day I broke, no physical space felt safe to me anymore, even though the problems I had were all virtual. My office felt poisoned and my home felt infiltrated and my friends seemed like enemies, all because there is no such thing as digital-only harassment – it bleeds into your life. I couldn't go to the office because it was on my work computer, and I couldn't go home because it was on my home computer, and I couldn't talk to my friends because they were all online and so they all knew about it, and they wanted to ask, with good intentions, "Doesn't it wear you down?" My answer, increasingly, was yes, of course it does.

I had tweeted earlier that morning that I wanted to read and commission more articles by non-white non-male writers. I was editing at the time, and the whitest, malest landscape in the country is long-form writing. This is boring, like offering the same selection of tooth-paste-flavoured ice cream for a century and then wondering why your business is failing. My version of media is one that looks like other people, because I remember being a little girl and wishing I read books or magazine articles or saw movies about people who even remotely looked like me. I became a writer because I read a David Sedaris book at thirteen; every word he wrote crackled in my brain, and he was a guy, sure, a white guy, but I knew he was different in a way that I felt different. Later that year, I read another book by an Indian writer about a first-generation Indian girl trying to date as a teenager, the plot alone blossoming in my heart when I read it. It changes you, when you see someone similar to you, doing the thing you might want to do yourself. That kind of writing – writing by people who aren't in the majority – its sheer visibility on your bookshelf or your television or your internet, is sometimes received similarly to my call for more of that work. It's responded to with racism or sexism or homophobia or transphobia. We are deeply afraid of making marginalized voices stronger, because we think it makes privileged ones that much weaker.

Maybe I was wrong and I shouldn't have said that I wanted more "non-white non-male writers." Maybe I should have said, "As much as I appreciate the contributions white men have made to the media landscape, and as much as I want to read another profile of a thin, blond actress where the writer quietly begs to have his virginity taken, that feels a little redundant, and maybe something worth examining." But you know what, I don't really give a shit. Those feelings are not my priority. That's kind of the point.

Media needs to diversify, and the only way to do that is to get non-white non-male non-binary people to work for and with you. It doesn't mean they're the only people you choose, but they are the ones we ignore the most. And when that message comes from a non-white non-male person themselves, someone young enough to not yet have any inherent gravitas and – this part is important – just enough privilege to be powerful, that's when they target you.

The response was fine, initially. I was handling it, the general misunderstanding of the worth of affirmative action. But then a few users twisted the knife and I started to get lightheaded. "Whites are literally GODS compared to all you shit colored freaks," wrote one user, and for some reason, it gave me pause. "Act like an insufferable cunt and then turn around and play the victim when people put you in your place," said another, and so I decided to go home early that day. "How many of your relatives are rapists? Hear that's pretty common in Asia" dropped into my feed. I hid under my covers, but I took my phone. Knowing what complete strangers were comfortable saying to me was one cruelty, but not knowing, and pretending that it didn't matter, was a worse kind of distress.

What followed were several days of rape threats, death threats, encouragements of suicide, racial slurs, sexist remarks, comments on my weight and appearance, attempts to get me fired or blacklisted, and even a quality jab about Hamhock failing to "civilize" me with his white penis. Nothing was unique, nothing was new, nothing unheard of. Calling me a cuckold and a bitch and a nigger, suggesting I should be raped by a beer bottle, followed home and attacked at night, or anally raped sans lubrication (*thank you for this elegant distinction, sir*) were hardly clever attacks.

Abstractly, the things they were saying meant nothing. There is no value, no consequence to someone calling me a dumb bitch. These people are the same ones who would be afraid of me if we ever met. But the volume of it was more than I could keep up with, the longest and largest and harshest string I'd faced. I was getting a few hundred notifications a day, all largely negative, all vaguely menacing. (Just vague enough, apparently, that Twitter did nothing to intervene.)

The internet used to be funny to me, this big global joke we were all in. Before, when I replied to users who, at their best, respectfully disagreed with me and, at their worst, wanted me murdered, it was a joke. It was a way to show how few emperors even owned clothes, never mind wore them. I thought we were laughing. I thought I was laughing. But after a few hours of answering and ironically engaging this time, I didn't find it funny, and Hamhock didn't find it funny, and my friends who were texting me, asking if I was having a very public meltdown, didn't find it funny. My dad, who found out about this spat of online harassment because a prominent international media organization wrote about it, did not find it funny. He called in near tears, trying to make sense of what Twitter was and why he couldn't read it himself. He wanted to see what people were saying, and I was thankful he couldn't.

I was still reading the comments and I replied to nearly every user, because hadn't they earned it? I had made myself available, and I had asked people to listen to me, so shouldn't I extend the same to someone who wanted me to miscarry a child I was not even bearing? It wasn't enough to exist online; I felt I had to engage because so many strangers demanded an answer. I owed them an answer. I was property, something entertaining or enticing or infuriating, but I was owned.

I refused to go to sleep unless my phone was glued to my hand so I could wake up at three in the morning and see if anyone had said something needlessly cruel about me. (They had.) I woke up the next morning and cried in bed while Hamhock rubbed my back and begged me to get up. He tried to tell me it wasn't real, but I knew it was, because we'd made extra sure to lock the back door in case someone decided, just once, to step away from their keyboard.

Throughout this ordeal I spoke with Jordan, who had since gone from being my boss to my friend. He was my first real editor at my first real job, the one who told me to write instead of hide, who rarely made eye contact for the first two years I worked with him but wrote me elegant emails telling me how to fix my work and how to be bolder. Jordan published my work, week after week, even when I didn't trust it and even when it felt risky. "It's good," he'd tell me through a thick beard, this assessment his highest bar for achievement. When the fallout would come, when people would come down hard on it or judge the work, based on my age or my gender, as futile and flimsy, he'd tell me to get off the internet and keep writing instead. He pulled some of my best work out of me, offline, in tangible places where his was the only voice I heard. Years ago, when another writer accused me of fabricating sources in my work, I went to Jordan, devastated and furious. "The thing to remember about him," he said, "is that he's nobody. Nobody at all. Fuck that guy in the ear."

Jordan is, in all the best ways, the opposite of me: he is incredibly calm, methodical, patient, and he can wait a full five minutes between a thought forming in his head and hurtling its way out of his mouth. When I worked for him, I used to sit on his desk and try to get him to talk because he is one of the few people I want to listen to. His online presence is sparing, detached, funny, and dry. But he is a man, a white man, who can get away with more than I could dream of. "There is no cowardice in removing yourself from a wildly unhealthy and unwinnable situation," he said when I told him about my Twitter account burning down before my eyes. "You shouldn't feel like you have to play." I complained about how unfair the world is, how hard it is to be a woman anywhere, how hard it is to be a non-white woman, how impossible it is to avoid getting the shit kicked out of you online for having an opinion, any opinion, and how resistant an entire industry is to positive change.

"I know," he said. "But you don't owe anyone anything. You don't have to be available to everyone. You can stop."

I deactivated my Twitter account that night.

If I were a beautiful person, a writer of beautiful things where everything ends with Our Noble Quirky Heroine learning a lesson about life, love, and the things that truly make us happy, I would have stayed off the internet for the rest of my life. I would be one of those people who eats

lunch alone in a crowded restaurant without even bringing my phone. I would go on vacation with every intention
of leaving my hotel room to learn some of the local language rather than staying inside to watch poorly translated reality television. I would make eye contact and I
would bake nut loaf and I would read books, like you are,
like some adorable idiot.

But, naturally, I did the opposite. I was furious that a
platform that felt like mine, that I had ownership of, was
ruined for me and people like me because a cabal of talking thumbs couldn't avoid calling me a bitch for more
than a single day. The worst part – if it's possible for us to
hit bottom in a bottomless pit filled with jagged anthropo-
morphic rocks chirping "BUT NOT ALL MEN" – is that the
treatment I received was still better than many have
experienced. I'm brown, but I have fair skin, I don't iden-
tify as queer or trans, I have no experience with visible
disabilities, and though I am the child of immigrants,
English is my first language. I am lucky, and I didn't
deserve half of it. No, I was right the first time: there is
no bottom. You just sink and sink and sink until the force
of your fall pulls the skin clean off your bones. I'd say it's
over before you know it, but I'm still waiting.

A small fraction of the internet took my departure
from Twitter as a statement. Four mainstream outlets
wrote about it, as did a few neo-Nazi blogs. I was either a
victim and a champion for women who get harassed
online, someone so strong and powerful that if I left,

there must really be a problem with the web, or I was a cunt who ran away when it got too hard to deal with.

But frankly, I just felt lonely. When I send my writing out into the world without checking Twitter, I'm left out of a conversation that I want to be in on. I want to know what I missed, what I fucked up, what I need to know for next time. I want to know that the work, hopefully, made you feel less lonely. Writing as one-way communication is rarely satisfying to me, probably because I've had some form of digital connection with the world and the strangers on it for most of my life. But with that comes a trove of unhelpful suggestions, attacks or attempts to demean my work for little reason other than people not liking me. If I want one, I have to have both, even if the conversation so frequently feels aggressive and cruel and destructive. I don't like feeling lonely.

Shutting off without warning was jarring and isolating, like having a friend you rely on just vanish with no explanation. Jordan was right: I didn't have to be there, be it for work or for personal gain. I didn't have to play. I realized, though, that I wanted to – I like attention and I like being able to control my own narrative. Above all, I like bothering people. I like being present in spaces where I am not welcome because you do not deserve to feel comfortable just because you're racist or sexist or small-minded. Something about ceding this territory, this part of the digital world that I felt ownership over, felt so deeply unfair. It's my house; why should I leave? I hated being offline, because I wasn't a martyr and I wasn't brave and I wasn't weak. I just didn't like the game, the rules of which I had helped write.

During my hiatus from Twitter I was hoping for some peace, for people to stop asking me if I was "doing okay" and to stop inserting themselves in what was salacious drama to them but structurally heartbreaking for me. But it was a lot like watching your own funeral. People I hated picked up the mantle and started advocating for me in a way I loathed, but I couldn't say anything because I was dead, remember? People who I thought were my friends (or whatever approximation of "friend" is possible if you met the person once at a crowded bar) turned against me as soon as it was clear I wouldn't retaliate. A former co-worker referred to me as a "tire fire" of a human being, and another acquaintance called me stupid and childish. Another established (Caucasian! Male!) national journalist said my call for writers was both "edgy" and a violation of human rights. (The Hague has yet to call.) Most didn't have much to say at all, because when you die, a shocking few will be sad. Once, when I thought I had embarrassed myself in front of a group of girls I was trying to impress, my then boyfriend told me, "You'd be shocked by how little people think about you." I broke up with him immediately, obviously, because everyone needs to look at me all the time, but it didn't make him wrong. No one cares more about your successes and your foibles than you.

This is the mistake I made. Everything felt personal. Every time I didn't like someone, I didn't like their character, I made them human and hated their humanity. I was irate when the "right" people didn't agree with me online, when I felt abandoned by people who should've said something, said it louder. But no one on the internet is actually a person; they're just an amalgamation of human parts, like a robot made from all the components of a person but missing the essentials, like a brain or a lymphatic system. It sounds like a person and, sometimes, looks like one, but it's not. It's an idea. You can't get mad at ideas as if they're people. An idea isn't going to hold your hand. Ideas don't owe you anything.

The harassment was bad, no question – and that's exactly what it was, a targeted attempt to make me question my physical and emotional safety. But it also had to do with my expectations. It's no wonder I keep fighting with riff-raff on the internet. I'm expecting human interaction, and all they're offering are beeps. I was dumb enough to want a hug from a machine.

After two weeks, I reactivated, the way anyone would: I posted a string of GIFs of noted wrestler The Undertaker coming back to life. The Undertaker popping out of a casket, The Undertaker reviving himself on the mat, The Undertaker running towards a large white man. The last one, perhaps my favourite: The Undertaker hanging his arms over the ropes, face bloodied, hair matted with sweat, barking defiantly, "This is my yard."

—

Solutions for how to handle social media tend to be all or nothing. You either succumb to the rules of the ruthless web, or you stay off it completely, out of fear or apathy or a refusal to let arbitrary arguments ruin your day. Neither option is realistic, and none are possible for women who rely on the internet for work or play. The platforms themselves hardly acknowledge that their infrastructure is a problem. At sixteen, we balked at Facebook because it wanted our real names and we still liked the perceived anonymity the internet gave us because it made it easier to be mean. Now, we still hate that we have to use our real names because it makes it easier for abusers and harassers to find us on yet another platform. (Some of us, with unusual monikers and silent letters and atypical spellings, for example, are even easier to find.) Twitter still can't agree on what harassing behaviour is, so while you might block or mute a person from your page, they can keep talking about you, keep sending their minions to flood your account, keep opening new accounts.

Plenty of us are fighting for structural changes, but a firmer solution has more to do with correcting human behaviour in general. No one learns how to be mean at twenty-five. No one actually becomes a hardline racist in their thirties. These are beliefs and behaviours we inherit from our bloodlines, from the people who raised us, and the internet is just another way to put those beliefs to work.

The troubling part is not that there are people online who feel comfortable – vindicated and strong – in calling me a cum-bucket. What scares me is that those people go out into the world, holding these convictions secretly or otherwise, and exist around me physically. I see them at the bank and they go to my dentist and I might end up working with them. What they say to me online is the purest distillation of the rage they feel – statements that would get them fired or arrested in real life but get them a moderate fan base or begrudging attention online. Maybe they consider their online presence a separate existence, but we all know it's the same person, no matter the platform.

We love to talk about the web as if it's a limitless resource, like the only barriers we put on it are what the government will allow, what money will buy, what man-power can create. But all things built by humans descend into the same pitfalls: loathing, vitriol, malicious intent. All the things we build in order to communicate, to con-nect, to find people like us so we feel less alone, and to find people not like us at all so we learn how to adapt, end up turning against us. Avoiding human nature at its most pure and even at its worst is pointless. No one deserves your attention, but no one has earned your withdrawal.

"Who do you even talk to on Twitter?" Papa asked me after I told him I had rejoined. "Who could be so import-ant there?" I thought about my family's traditional Kashmiri last name, how any other Kashmiri can point us out in a phone book and know where we're from. This has, literally, happened: when I was still living at home, a recent immigrant looked up our listed number, called us, and asked if he could come over to talk to my parents and get some help integrating. Mom made him fried vangan and Papa offered him chai and I was perplexed that my otherwise very private, very protective parents let a complete stranger stroll into their home just because he came from the same region they did. But they were trying to find connection, to talk to someone who understood them. I will likely have to tell you, here, that vangan is eggplant, but online, I can find someone in mere seconds who already knows that. Our worlds become a little smaller, we feel closer, we feel less alone.

Eventually, that interaction won't merit abuse online. It won't result in a skinhead sending me a message about how brown people smell like shit, or how we should be thanking white people for allowing us to live here. But that pendulum doesn't swing if you detach, if you refuse to play entirely, if you leave the room and try to play by yourself.

Papa, after accepting that I returned to Twitter, abruptly stopped speaking to me when his feathers were re-ruffled by my decision, his go-to when he's too overwhelmed to even be mad. I tweeted, "An amazing thing about brown parents is they can be mad at you, get over it, and a year later, decide they are not done being mad at you." My mentions filled with responses, little hearts signifying that others agreed; "omg yes" wrote one woman

Papa <papa@gmail.com>, August 27, 2015
Did she pay for the lunch?

Scaachi <sk@gmail.com>, August 27, 2015
why are you obsessed with whether people buy me lunch or not
i am not destitute

Papa <papa@gmail.com>, August 27, 2015
If they do that means they hold you in high esteem ok omg

a better person. This, of all years, will be the year you are not walking acid reflux, where you take care of yourself, where you will floss. I was only asking four weeks of sobriety for and from myself, just thirty-one days, though I'd never gone that long without a glass of wine since I started drinking. My trip would be self-indulgent enough, complete with what the locals call a Bucket of Joy: ice, Red Bull, Sprite, and rum or whisky. It's a death wish served in a frosty pail, and I was going to drink all of them.

Before I would get there, however, I'd drain my body of its toxins, eat right, go to the gym, and drink plenty of water. I'd talk about yoga. (I wouldn't, like, go to yoga, but I'd talk about it. If I've learned anything from white women, it's that the best kind of yoga is the kind you talk about fucking constantly.)

It's not that I drink a lot. I rarely drink during the week, and my weekend drinking generally consists of juuuust enough wine to make me forget about the three times I've accidentally sent my boss a furious and deeply intimate Facebook message intended for Hamhock. But I like alcohol because it induces a kind of stupor I can control, one that comes in gentle waves, that I can keep at bay with water and disco fries or make harsher with amber-coloured liquor. Booze has, probably, played a bigger part in my life than I ever intended. (Though what is a "normal" amount of alcohol for someone with a baseline level of childhood trauma? Is it worse if I rim a Tom Collins with crushed Children's Tylenol? LET ME LIVE.) My birthdays get increasingly foggy thanks to pinot over dinner; good news is celebrated with off-brand champagne. ("You can't call it champagne if it's not *from* Champagne," Hamhock says as I try to saw his head off with a broken bottle.) Every important relationship I've had has been formed over a beer. Hamhock and I met at a kegger hosted by his friend in a dimly lit backyard. I went with my best friend, and while Hamhock failed to persuade me to do a keg stand, my buddy did it twice while I held his glasses. I poured him into a cab at two in the morning as he purred a pitiful, "You're a good egg." Alcohol is the great equalizer. Alcohol makes you brave. Alcohol makes you beautiful. Alcohol makes you fall in love.

I didn't grow up in a home with much alcohol consumption. Mom gets loaded from one or two glasses of very tart white wine, and Papa will have a Scotch merely, I think, because he likes saying, "Gimme two fingers!" while holding up his index and pinky, five inches apart. (Then he laughs, which is your cue to also laugh.) He becomes gregarious for an hour and then calls it a night. I didn't drink much in high school either, missing that phase where everyone discovers how sexy and touchable they are when they nurse four ounces of warm raspberry Sour Puss in a red party cup. I went to one house party at seventeen, a month after graduation, drank two Smirnoff Ices, and wondered where everyone's parents were.

When I moved to Toronto for university, I was still two years younger than the legal drinking age. I didn't move into a residence but, rather, into a Best Western hotel where five floors were converted into student housing. The beds had been taken out and two small plastic cots were installed, with a flimsy plastic barrier between them to offer some semblance of privacy from the stranger sleeping four feet from your head. My roommate was a Chinese exchange student who told me, repeatedly, her name was Alice, but she carried around books and paperwork with the name Mia scrawled on them. (Alice/Mia vanished without notice after the first semester, leaving behind only a pair of broken flip-flops.) The rest of the building otherwise still functioned as a hotel, so while tourists checked in to this crumbling, unkempt building sandwiched between what was then the city's oldest gay bathhouse and a private middle school filled with teens who owned Amexes, a few hundred seventeen-, eighteen-, nineteen-, and twenty-year-olds were getting fucked up. We attempted to break into the pool (which was off limits), and tried to pry our eleventh-floor windows open to throw pennies at pedestrians.

That Best Western was where I learned how to drink. In high school, I was too paranoid my parents would show up and force their fingers down my throat to make me vomit the puddles of beer I choked down. But here, here I could be fun without threat of retribution. And I was learning that I needed to be fun if I was going to get anyone to talk to me.

When you're a girl, you learn pretty fast that boys will like you if you can drink. Not if you will drink, but if you can drink like the boys and hold it together. Girls don't get to be sloppy, they don't get to boot 'n rally. They have to be buzzed, perpetually, while still keeping up, playing beer pong, taking shots, being fuckable, being fun. The first adult I ever had a crush on – five years older than me, with skin so white I wanted to ruin it with crayons – once told me, "You can really drink for a girl." It was a badge of honour. Later, he amended it: "I've never seen a brown girl drink like you can." He was impressed. I was impressive. I was fun. And I felt brave. Drinking does that, makes you feel like you can crush the world under your heel, or possibly seduce it into submission.

But girls don't actually get to drink like boys because boys do things to girls when they drink. When I was a teenager, the world told me that a girl is responsible for her own body if she's raped or assaulted when she's drunk: that's her fault, it's on her to not get so drunk she stops being fun and starts being a liability. My parents always told me drinking was risky, that it opened up the recesses of a man's brain and made him primal and territorial. Of course that's bad, we were told, but it's up to you to keep yourself safe. For the first few weeks at the hotel, when I was invited to different parties in different dorm rooms, when older students offered to buy drinks for me, I attended reluctantly, in bulky clothes and with unbrushed hair. I refused to let anyone touch my drink, no one could open a beer for me, no one was allowed to offer me a cup, even an empty one – I'd bring my own. I was learning how to be fun, sure, but the threat loomed: one of the guys here can take it away from you in a heartbeat, and it'll be your fault.

I missed university orientation when I moved, so I started classes knowing no one except a vegan girl in my program who also happened to live down the hall from me. (She would not be a friend. I and a few boys in the dorm borrowed a dormmate's bearskin rug, draped it over ourselves, and stormed into her room to scare her.)

But within the first few weeks, I met Jeff, a rowdy boy a year older than me who wore old T-shirts unironically and looked like he could lift a car over his head. I hated him immediately: he was loud and self-confident and in the middle of the day – sober, I figured – he was fun, and that just seemed unfair. He was from Canada's farmland, a verified country bro who, had he gone to my high school, would have been polite but unfeeling towards me. Jeff came with another boy, a narrow-faced, skinny-legged seventeen-year-old named Matt Braga. I hated him more than I hated Jeff: he was weaselly and had saucer-eyeballs that bulged when he caught you in a mistake, and if you asked him a question, he'd lean back in his chair and fold his arms and say, "Aaaaaahhhhhmmmm," before answering. He looked like a baby so I called him effortlessly smart so we didn't have to listen, or sat in the front of the class, to prove we knew everything already. We were where the party was, for once meaning I wasn't chasing a party or searching for the right place to be: we *were* the place to be. Baby Braga, too, got wrapped up in how much your life changes when you're given permission to be young and selfish. People texted *us*, for once, asking where we were and if they could come. Braga was erudite, hardly a risk-taker, a little shy and plenty anxious. I was too, but with Jeff, we got to be whatever we wanted. I didn't watch my drinks anymore, or worry about other men, because Jeff did it for me. We went to a nightmare bar off campus called Dance Cave where girls barfed in plastic cups on the floor and Braga's glasses slipped off his face and were stomped by moving feet. Jeff and I spent weeks trying to teach Baby Braga how to smoke a cigarette without looking like he was fellating a corn dog. (We never succeeded.) We got to be versions of ourselves that somehow existed in a parallel universe where we were fun.

It took Braga and me far longer to become friends than it took either of us to fall in love with Jeff — but how could you resist Jeff? He was intoxicating, so comfortable shirking responsibility and making you feel like it was the most important thing in the world that you came to this party, like there would never be another one. Baby Braga and I, rather, found each other through beer and Canadian Club after a few months. At yet another party at Jeff's, we wound up alone in a bedroom and fell backwards on the bed, laughing at something I can't remember. The lights were dim and our eyes locked, so this was where we were supposed to kiss and ruin everything. Instead, we started laughing maniacally, tears welling up, his voice getting raspy from screaming. "Come on, idiot," I said, pulling him up by the forearm and leading him back into the kitchen to find some plastic cups for an unnecessary drinking game. (Who needs a game to drink?)

I liked hanging out with Jeff and Baby Braga, partly because spending time with boys was once verboten. Any brown girl can tell you that if you come home with a male friend, your father will kick you out of the house, give you the silent treatment for an indeterminate period of time, or try to hex you in public. Your mother, meanwhile, will weep in the attic. (This is true even if you do not have an attic.) The three of us walked around campus together, went to bars together, had hungover brunches together, a team in perfect synergy where the most important things were each other and then, also, having a good time. We locked arms and marched into the world and we loved each other.

We were invincible thanks to the poisonous combination of youth and loneliness and the drinks that tethered us together. And we really did love drinking, particularly since it allowed us to press a kind of reset button, gave us some psychic break from our lives before starting over in earnest. We could make everything blur together, get ourselves low enough, and tomorrow could be something new entirely. And we figured this would last forever, the three of us, regardless of how our lives would shift. "Everyone's the worst!" we'd chant, toasting our pint glasses to solidify our bond and rejecting everyone else.

After nights like these, Baby Braga and I would call each other and recount the night before. Jeff, often, was still asleep.

"What happened to Jenna?" I'd ask him.

"She hit her head on the edge of the stove in the kitchen. She was bleeding really badly," he'd tell me. "I think she went to the hospital."

We laughed because she was surely okay so it was still fun. It was fun that Jeff wouldn't wake up until two in the afternoon and then he'd text us, "Brunch?" and we'd laugh because, oh, Jeff, you doofus, it's two in the afternoon, and you missed all your classes! Later that night, we'd meet up with him and he'd already have two drinks in his system and he'd pick me up and spin me around. He and Baby Braga would sing karaoke sans karaoke machine. He gave me a key to the apartment he shared with four other people (a two-floor rental with two decks, a cavernous kitchen, and a whisper of a bathroom) who were all fun like Jeff, so I came and went as I pleased. One morning I was sitting in the kitchen trying to clean the mess from the night before and Jeff walked in with crate after crate of home-brewed wine. It tasted like toilet juice and it didn't even last a week.

Another night, Jeff climbed onto the roof of that apartment, jumping from building to building, screaming into the darkness. It was one in the morning and we kept yelling back at him, "You're going to get arrested!" but we were laughing because this moron never got in trouble. Jeff could have ten drinks and run a marathon, in the dark, sleep-deprived, on rooftops in east downtown. When he finally came back, he pretended to chase me and I pretended to be afraid.

This was our routine for more than two years, but the unsustainable part of our plan was that Jeff never stopped at one or two or three drinks, he always needed to get to ten or fifteen or twenty. When he drank like that, he'd stop singing and sit in his bedroom, slumped over in old clothes, near tears. Baby Braga would try to drag him to Wing Machine to eat something, sober up a little, and when that failed he'd try again the next day. Because this was the point, right? You can always start over the next day.

By the time we were in our third year, Jeff started to forget things, started to shrink. His shoulders were more sloped. He lost so much weight that he was punching new holes in his belts to keep his pants up, and his T-shirts looked like parachutes. He drank faster and harder than us, getting too drunk to walk me home like he used to. Once, I walked home alone at the crack of dawn and was grabbed by a man who tried to throw me to the ground. A passerby chased him off and escorted me the rest of the way, but when I called Jeff in tears, he didn't answer. The next day, he apologized profusely, saying his girlfriend had been over and they were fighting and he didn't have his phone. "I don't know about that," Baby Braga told me. "I mean, he passed out while I was still there. He was pretty drunk." I didn't want to be his burden, his responsibility, because fun girls aren't needy. We had been doing this for years, consequence-free, and being a woman never changed how I drank around these boys. Baby Braga sometimes walked me home, or texted me to make sure I got back okay after long nights. We were still okay.

But sometimes, Jeff would climb back onto his roof and threaten to kill himself – Braga and I were never sure whether he meant it – and I'd reach my hand up to try and grab his withering arm. "Come on," I'd say. "Come inside. Let's make martinis. Let's have some wine. We can play a drinking game. Come into the kitchen." He'd nod and smile and swing his legs down but he never really came back to us. He circulated through his own party like a ghost, too drunk to play and too sad to stop.

Jeff chipped his tooth one evening in a series of mysterious events Baby Braga and I couldn't sort out. He came to class smelling like old cigarette smoke, and the tips of his fingers were turning grey. During breaks, he'd go outside to smoke and glare at the pavement in silence. We watched him from the windows, surly and disconnected, rubbing his eyes and tensing his jaw. At Thanksgiving, he tried to get in a fist fight with all the people he'd invited over for lasagna and gutter wine. I left early, one of the first times a party didn't interest me as much as being away from it did. Baby Braga texted me that Jeff ripped his shirt off and fell off the roof. But it was okay, because Jeff was our friend, he was just a lot of fun! He would be okay because he had us. Of *course* a troop of teenagers had the cure for what was possibly a young alcoholic spinning out of control. We would be fine!

I wondered if other people noticed, but how could they not? We were noticing. It was the only thing Baby Braga and I talked about now. Our pal, our passport into a good party, was increasingly a liability. While everyone else we knew was starting to shake off the near-nightly drinking, the back-alley smoking, the endless hot-boxing of bedrooms and bathrooms, Jeff was still there. "Come over," he'd text me on a Tuesday night. "Let's have a few." I'd say no because I had class the next day and I just wanted to stay home. He wouldn't talk to me for a day or two after, and when he'd eventually come around, he was still angry. "I can't believe you didn't come over!" he said. "You missed so much fun."

By then, most of us were legal drinking age, so the conceit of drowning our evenings and weekends (and sometimes, days) in alcohol appealed to Baby Braga and me less and less. He started calling me – on the phone, something no other nineteen-year-old has ever done barring a physical emergency – to see what I was up to. "Do you want to have dinner?" replaced "What bar are we going to?" Braga and

SCAACHI KOUL

I met for towering sandwiches and weird burgers and simmering plates of cheap Thai food and we talked instead of screamed. We drank coffee. "Jeff's okay, right?" I'd ask him, and he'd shrug, saying, "How would we even know?"

Baby Braga and I pleaded with Jeff to sober up, just go cold turkey. You can do it, we told him, we'll help you. Braga talked to him Like A Man, whatever that means, and tried to reassure him that we'd still be around, even when the party was over. I told him that our lives would open up, that maybe the three of us could get an apartment and live together and it would be weird and delightful. Jeff was always drunk when we had these conversations, so he'd hang his head and nod and quietly let a tear drop from his lashes onto his sock. Baby Braga and I kept hanging out with him all the same, kept going to the parties, trying to keep our little world from combusting. Except now, Braga walked me home much earlier.

After nearly three years of being together, our chaos at first joyful and later, muted, Jeff returned from a brief vacation and met me at a frat party. I ran at him and threw myself into his arms for a hug, because it was just us this time. Baby Braga wasn't around, so it was up to me to keep him alive, keep him bright. He was already drunk, but he was at that perfect place where he wasn't sullen and dark but gregarious and friendly. He picked me up, just barely, because he wasn't as strong as he used to be. "Missed you, kid," he said, because I was always little when we were together.

[152]

We didn't know anyone else at the party, so we drank together. But his mood shifted, because his mood always shifted, and he sat in a leather armchair in the corner and refused to talk. I had plenty of watery beer and lost my temper – one of the many things girls aren't allowed to do when they drink – and started yelling at him over the music. "What is wrong with you?" I asked. "Just stop drinking. No one's making you do this. No one's asking you to come out for this." The frat had changed all their light bulbs to red, making everything look like blood and panic. "You have a problem," I cried. He refused to speak to me until I dragged him to an empty room, a quiet place to talk away from the party.

We fought more, him mostly listening and me mostly yelling. But eventually Jeff rose from the thin mattress he was seated on, reminding me that he was a good foot taller than I am. He grabbed me with the hands he always did, the ones that cracked open twist-offs or shoved other men away from me or wrapped around my own to pull me through a crowd when I got lost, but this time, he gripped and shook my body like he hadn't before. I closed my mouth and watched his face twist with unknown rage and then fall, his eyes widened, welling with tears, his face flushing a deeper shade of red than the lighting already made it. I felt exposed, rattled, his body hanging over me like a threat I always knew loomed. I was scared. It was too intimate a transgression, a clear violation that I could finally read. It was the least fun we had ever had together.

Women can't be fun all the time, can't drink without
consequence. Frankly, few people can, but who feels the
consequences of their otherwise harmless actions quite
like women? People told me countless times how dangerous it is to be a woman and drink near men, how careful
you have to be, how it's your fault if you let something
happen. Papa hates hearing stories about my alcohol consumption, certain that it speaks to my lack of safety away
from him. Maybe he's right. But I didn't wrap his fingers
around my arm, I didn't rattle my own frame. I had moved
out of my parents' house years ago, but when I returned to
my apartment later that night, and walked into my closet
and closed the door – something I did as a kid when I got
in trouble, a way to feel shame in private – I was homesick.
I cried and wished my mother was in the other room, ready
to run her long nails across my scalp to calm me down.

A week later, I stormed into his apartment with the
key he had given me and took all the booze from his
apartment – some of it not even his – and threw it in the
dumpster outside his house. I threw the key at him and
cried and he begged me to stop screaming and said he
would try to be a better person. "I just need one more weekend," he said. He wanted one more bender for his birthday.

I cut him out on the night of his twentieth.

It's amazing what you can convince yourself of when you
think everyone else is beneath you. I felt great during the

Your life's greatest heartbreaks are so often your friends: dating isn't always built for permanence, but friendship often is. You lose a lot of friends after university, more if you take an active stance against someone who used to be in the group. Worse is when those friendships are the ones you make when you move somewhere new and try on a new identity for a while, something that you think will fit better, will make people like you, and it still doesn't work. After you shoot out into the world and build a community, and people leave, you feel the loneliest you've ever been in your life. The formula doesn't work, and the people you think you'll love forever when you're eighteen and you've had too much to drink are rarely around when you need them. The University Friend exists in only one ecosystem, a relationship that requires the confines of a school, of a space in time where you are lost and digging for belonging, where your identity is so scattered you're just happy to be loved. Drinking is fun, but it's also the glue that holds you and your most tenuous connections together.

Jeff was more fun than me, so when we stopped speaking, plenty of other people stopped talking to me. Baby Braga and I watched our friends forget my birthday but never miss one of Jeff's ragers, screen my texts but go for late-afternoon brunch at Jeff's house, ignore us on New Year's, Halloween, St. Patrick's Day – the early-twenties holiday starter pack – to see him instead. When they heard about what had happened at the frat party, they asked me if I was sure, if I was drinking too, if I was maybe being too hard on him. Aren't I typically hysterical, don't I have tendencies towards dramatics? Baby Braga, meanwhile, came with me in the divorce, another untouchable by association. We didn't host parties and we didn't have fun follow us. I reminded them that their fun friend would eventually be thirty – old! – and his drinking would soon look less like a glamorous scene and more like an unfixable calamity. I reminded them how sad our little world was, but the ecosystem won out.

A year after I stopped going to the parties and stopped taking Jeff's calls, Baby Braga invited me to his new apartment for mac 'n' cheese and his preferred type of beer: bitter, hoppy, almost undrinkable, sure to send me into an inconsolable rage. ("This tastes like twigs!" I'll say and he'll say "I like it!" and I'll ask "But why?" and he'll say "Well, I'm sorry it's not a *gin and tonic*" with this very precise derision where he extends all the vowels and raises his eyebrows above his glasses and then I will try to strangle him.)

"You know," I told him, "we don't hear from anyone anymore."

"I know," he said. "They all just disappeared. What happened?"

"I left."

"I guess I did too."

Baby Braga shovelled pasta shells filled with creamy cheese into a bowl for me while I started to cry on his

couch, something I did all the time, almost every weekend, because I was alone.

"I don't think you should feel bad about it," he said,
putting a warm bowl in my lap and handing me a napkin
for my face and for the food I would inevitably spill on
his couch. "I mean, I'm still around."

The second weekend of Dry January, I came home on
Friday night after a trying week of yet again aggressively emailing my editor, "You are such a fucking asshole," intended for an unnecessary fight with Hamhock.
I thought again about Jeff, this idiot who broke up our
triad. I had a choice between dealing with his drunken
memory bashing itself against the walls of my sober
brain, or meeting Baby Braga for a drink at a nearby
bar. I wanted to make it through the month sober, but I
missed Jeff — even at his most destructive — like a dull
ache I couldn't soothe. I still take Braga with me almost
everywhere I go, refusing to go through any significant
life changes or emotional turmoil without his presence,
but Jeff was our third. It had taken us years to recalibrate.
When we left him for good, I considered it his punishment. He would be alone, karmic payback for the night
he grabbed me. He'd understand that he didn't deserve
us. Maybe he'd feel so bad about it that one day he'd get
his shit together and call me and we'd all try again. I
was so angry, years later, again, angry like I was when

he first rattled me with his paws, proof positive that there were no truly safe spaces.

I drained my fury by filling up with liquid poison. I'd made it sixteen days without a drink. While watching Braga force a pulled pork sandwich into his tiny rabbit mouth, I drank three beers in forty minutes and noticed, somehow for the first time, just how often I use alcohol to drown out regret.

The morning after I failed Dry January, I woke with a headache and my mouth like a desert, a hangover as punishment for fucking up my one sober month. I thought about emailing Jeff to say I was sorry for being so harsh, that I'd failed him, and that I hoped he was okay, whatever that means. I wanted to yell at him, too, blame him for hurting me and ruining our bubble, even if it was impossible to maintain forever. I knew his aggression wasn't just about drinking but about something more primal in his brain, something that lashed out at a woman he said he loved. And yet, I felt guilty for not trying even harder than I already had. Maybe I abandoned him, maybe *we* abandoned him. I had been angry for myself for such a long time that I forgot to be sad for him.

But Baby Braga called me first, so instead, I listened to him chirp about ice skating and being at the grocery store, reminding me that today, like all days, wasn't the day before. I didn't ask about Jeff because it didn't matter: that world was long dead and I missed it only in hindsight, where the things you lost clutter up your head on bad days. Braga and I dragged each other out of our old microcosm, enough of a victory for me. "What day is it?" he asked me. I could hear him crinkling a bag in the background while I restarted my process of shaking off the night before, pulling the covers off my head and taking a deep drink of water. "These bagels go bad in, like, seven days. I love bagels. They are my one true vice. It's fine, I'll buy them next week. Are you free this — *ooh, Sriracha* — are you free this week? Let's hang out. We'll get sandwiches and tea and catch up properly. It'll be fun."

Scaachi <sk@gmail.com>, April 30, 2013
my boss called me competent today

Papa <papa@gmail.com>, April 30, 2013
That warms the coccles of my heart.
Were his lips a bit curled when he said this. I do not trust
anybody.

Hunting Season

———

Recently, like on so many of my best weekends, I went out with a few friends for a couple of drinks that instead ended up turning into about ten drinks each. We had all attended an awards ceremony earlier in the evening, where I had, deservedly, lost, so we went to a nearby bar and drank warmly with each other. Baby Braga put his hand on my shoulder and said, "Heeey, paaaal," his marquee greeting for, "I am too drunk to say anything else." Jordan was there too, and let me lean on his tall frame as I teetered on heels that pinched my toes but made me feel older than I was. By two-thirty in the morning we were all drunk, and it was drunkenness that I wore on my face: I was laughing at my own jokes and my eyelids were dipping and the pincurls I had done earlier that night were starting to sag.

The boys and I stood by the bar and talked. Two men sitting near us looked over at me periodically and laughed to each other. They were talking louder than they realized, discussing how drunk I seemed, how I was clearly out of my mind. They talked about how many more drinks I might need before I could be approached, before one of them could take me home to sleep with me. They posited how many drinks I'd need to put out.

I tugged at Jordan and Braga and tried to explain what was happening, but it was clear I wasn't making any sense to them: Jordan just frowned at me, and Braga, properly imbibed himself, just groaned, "Paaaaaaal." So instead of continuing to try to explain, I begged them not to leave me alone, not to go to the bathroom, not to go outside for a cigarette without me. We stayed together for the rest of the night, and my friend Danny escorted me right to my front door, twenty-piece chicken nugget meal tucked under my arm, fifteen sweet-and-sour sauce packets hidden in my bra.

A few weeks before that, I'd gone to dinner with another friend. We ordered a second bottle of wine for ourselves, a typical routine for us. (She once told me to start drinking rosé because it's "a literary drink," which is maybe the best excuse I've ever heard to start drinking something new.) When the bottle arrived and we let out a delighted laugh, we noticed two men seated near us lean in and say to each other: "We're in." We grimaced and drank our bottle, then a third after that.

Years before that, when I was just barely old enough to get into a bar and order a drink, a man had offered to buy me a drink. I said no, no thank you, I'd just got one. He was hitting on me, clearly, but I didn't realize that, so naturally he tensed up and got angry at me, the way any good guy would. "What are you even here for?" he said, picking up his ball and going home.

Often, people describe rape as an unfortunate accident, two drunk bodies colliding: it's more about miscommunication than intentionally ignoring a lack of consent, or actively seeking a body and mind that can't say no. But rape culture doesn't flourish by error; it's a methodical operation so ingrained in our public consciousness that we don't even notice when it's happening, and we rarely call it out even when we do see it.

Men watch women in a way we've long since normalized. It's normal for men to watch you when you enter a bar, to watch what you're drinking, what you're doing, in an attempt to get closer to you. It's normal for them to offer you a drink, and when you say no, to press a little further with are you sure, come on, have one drink with me. (When a guy asks to buy you a drink, suggest he buy you a snack instead and see how that goes over.) Men watch women at the gym, at work, on the subway: in any space occupied by men and women, the women are being watched.

The men seated next to me at the bar recently weren't trying to figure out how to talk to me. They weren't discussing what would work as a good opening line or how to impress me so I would willingly go home with one of them. They weren't even deciding whether they wanted to buy me a drink or what I actually needed, which was a burrito. They were conspiring.

Have you heard of "party culture"? It's one of many false culprits that rapists blame for their actions, as if party culture influences them to assault an unconscious or drunk woman. Brock Turner, the Stanford swimmer found guilty in 2016 of sexual assault, argued that alcohol and party culture were to blame for what he did to a drunk, unconscious woman. It somehow strips away every modicum of morality or ethics you have. It's not his fault; it's just that they were both drunk.

Turner's blaming booze is hardly the first time alcohol has been considered a bigger factor in an assault than the formulaic, intentional calculation of a rapist. In 2012, seventeen-year-old Rehtaeh Parsons, of Dartmouth, Nova Scotia, killed herself after she was gang-raped while intoxicated and the photos of the assault were circulated online. That same year, in Steubenville, Ohio, a high school girl was raped by her classmates while she was drunk, then photographed. In 2013, Vanderbilt University football players were accused of raping an unconscious twenty-one-year-old student in a dorm.

What a coincidence that rapists so frequently seem to find women who are drunk.

We know being drunk doesn't mean you deserve to be assaulted, and we know that there are plenty of men who can drink without raping someone. When we think of rape, we tend to think of coordinated calculation: Men who drive around in unmarked vans with duct tape and chloroform in the back. Men who follow women around, tracking their daily moves, catching them at their most vulnerable. We think of rape in terms of how men create intricate plans for hurting women, for sexual violence at its most gruesome, men who use physical force to hold women down. But we don't, for some reason, associate it with a man who surveils you in public, maybe for an hour or two, to see if you're getting drunk on your own or if he needs to help you along by buying you a drink. These types of rapes — rapes where women are too drunk to consent, or unconscious, or when no one bothers to ask for consent in the first place — are considered accidents. Everyone was in the wrong place at the wrong time. Youthful indiscretion. Party culture. It's the wine's fault. We forget that there's calculation, that he walked up to you because you were teetering and he thought it would be easy.

Pickup-artist culture is most obviously dedicated to monitoring women, to tracking their moves and how the little ways we let our guard down may benefit a man. Roosh V, a pickup artist perhaps best known for saying rape should be legal, gives tips on his site for which girls you should pick up at a bar: "I look for girls who are drinking . . . It's possible to have a one-night stand with a sober girl, but a few drinks in her makes it easier."

But we see it in far less insidious places too, normalized in what we consume as entertainment. On the U.S. version of *The Office*, Michael Scott spent much of the first few episodes sexually harassing his boss, Jan, ignoring her when she said no and following her around. After a night of drinking, they slept together, but she still rejected him the next day. He continued to harass her at work and monitor her actions to see if something suggested she didn't mean it when she said no. *How I Met Your Mother*'s Barney Stinson had pickup techniques that, if displayed in the real world, would get him arrested. Plenty of *Mad Men* episodes were about getting women drunk in order to take them home.

Surveillance feeds into rape culture more than drinking ever could. It's the part of male entitlement that makes them believe they're owed something if they pay enough attention to you, monitor how you're behaving to see if you seem loose and friendly enough to accommodate a conversation with a man you've never met. He's not a rapist. No, he's just offering to buy you a beer, and a shot, and a beer, and another beer, he just wants you to have a really good time. He wants you to lose the language of being able to consent. He's drunk too, but of course, you're not watching him like he's watching you.

The first time I was roofied, I was barely eighteen, and as I walked home from one bar I was swept into another by a man who promised me a glass of water and a comfortable seat. "I'll get you some water and then you'll be able to get home okay," he told me. I said okay because I didn't have the language for, "No, please get me a cab." He was nice to me and he had a soft, French accent and he was cute. (I think he was cute. I just remember a vague brunette blob holding my hand and guiding me to a table.)

He put a glass in front of me and I drank greedily, until my brain got foggier and my limbs felt weak. He sat next to me for most of the night, he watched me tip the glass to my mouth, he waited for my words to become more and more indistinct. He turned his back for a second and I stole away to the bathroom because I knew something was wrong with my body, knew that my brain couldn't send a message to my legs to stop shaking or my heart to beat slower. It was a distress signal I had heard about from other women who always told me to be careful with my drinks, to cover them up, to drink out of bottles if possible, to avoid a drink that might be fizzing unnecessarily. It was the first time, and yet, familiar: I caught a glimpse of myself in the bathroom mirror – hair matted, forehead beaded with sweat, lips dry and cracked – before my legs locked and I collapsed.

Outside the door, a woman heard me fall, and she came in and picked me up. She asked me what my name was and where I lived and I don't remember telling her anything. She carried me out front, through a snowbank, and into a cab. The guy who had spent the night with me, who was running around the bar trying to find me, rushed up before she could close the door. "Wait," he said, "she's with me. I'll take her home."

The woman turned to him, blocking me from his view. "Okay," she said. "What's her name?"

My name is difficult enough for the sober, for people I have known for years, never mind a stranger at a bar, someone who I do not think ever asked me what my name was. He backed off immediately, and the woman handed my cab driver some money and put my seatbelt on for me. "Take her straight home and make sure she gets inside," she said. "And if you don't, I will find out, because I'm a lawyer." I woke up the next morning on my kitchen floor in my penguin pyjama bottoms.

The second time, a bartender drugged both me and my (male) friend. Our best theory is that he was trying to get to me, and that was easier if my friend was out of commission. We were both dizzy and hysterical and con- fused after two drinks apiece. I walked him to the subway at midnight and remember nothing else, except that he lost his phone and we were both sick for days. I laughed it off—"I've done this before," I told him—but he was so rattled he didn't ask to see me for months.

Both times, I knew I was being watched. The first time, I was being watched when I stumbled down a street by myself, and so I got pulled into a bar I didn't want to go into. I was watched while I drank, watched while I struggled to give answers. My drunkenness was monitored, because the drunker I got, the less resistance I could offer. Saying no is a clear full stop, but if I can't really speak at all, if my words are running together and I'm closer to sleep than struggle, then it's somehow okay to take me home.

The second time, I was being watched by a bartender who spent too much time hovering over our drinks, who filled them up from an area behind the bar I couldn't see. Who knew I had to be wary of the guy whose job it was to give me a drink and, preferably, not poison me? If you can't trust your bartender, you can't trust anyone.

And yet, being surveilled with the intention of assault or rape is practically mundane, it happens so often. It's such an ingrained part of the female experience that it doesn't register as unusual. The danger of it, then, is in its routine, in how normalized it is for a woman to feel monitored, so much so that she might not know she's in trouble until that invisible line is crossed from "typical patriarchy" to "you should run."

So now, when I drink, I'm far more cautious. I don't like ordering draft beers from taps hidden from view. I don't like pouring bottles into pint glasses. I don't leave my drink with strangers, I don't let people I don't know order drinks for me without watching them do it, and I don't drink excessively with people I don't think I can trust with my sleepy body. I don't turn my back on a cocktail, not just because I like drinking but because I can't trust what happens to it when I'm not looking. The intersection of rape culture and surveillance culture means that being a guarded drinker is not only my responsibility, it is my *sole* responsibility. Any lapse in judgment could not only result in clear and present danger, but also set me up for a chorus of "Well, she should've known better."

The mistake we make is in thinking rape isn't premeditated, that it happens by accident somehow, that you're drunk and you run into a girl who's also drunk and half-asleep on a bench and you sidle up to her and things get out of hand and before you know it, you're being accused of something you'd never do. But men who rape are men who watch for the signs of who they believe they can rape. Rape culture isn't a natural occurrence; it thrives thanks to the dedicated attention given to women in order to take away their security. Rapists exist on a spectrum, and maybe this attentive version is the most dangerous type: women are so used to being watched that we don't notice when someone's watching us for the worst reason imaginable. They have a plan long before we even get to the bar to order our first drink.

Papa <papa@gmail.com>, March 3, 2016

I'm a big fan of Suge Knight.

He upset the humdrum routine of everyday life.

Scaachi <sk@gmail.com>, March 3, 2016

He might be a murderer.

Papa <papa@gmail.com>, March 3, 2016

Murder is necessary to social order.

Mister Beast Man to You, Randor

———

The most terrifying prospect that comes with learning about oral sex is appreciating that someday you might want to let someone's face be that close to your vagina. With their mouth. Their *mouth*.

I was eleven or twelve when I learned about oral sex, and I hadn't even looked directly at my vagina yet. It would be another year before I'd take my mom's old compact mirror, pull back the folds, and try to make sense of what was going on down there. I'm supposed to let a man put his mouth on this? Does he blow into the hole? What if I pee directly into his mouth? *Oh my god, does he pee into the hole?* What kind of laughable hellscape is womanhood supposed to be?

This horror was just the first in a long string of miserable realizations, which came around the time I noticed
that my body made me different from the girls at school
I considered attractive. My skin was darker than that of
my female peers, and my body wasn't shaped like a white
girl's — I had thick arms and dark knuckles and ashy
knees. My lips were full (not trendy quite yet) and the
bridge of my nose was wide and broken. When I played
with the other girls, they got to be Mary Jane and I was,
inexplicably, Spider-Man: not normal enough to be
human, not cool enough to be a worthy superhero.

Puberty hit fast and ugly. Almost overnight, I looked
over the expanse of my body and noticed sharp, dark,
thick hairs sprouting all over me. I was covered in hair by
the sixth grade, with a unibrow forming, my arms already
furry and my legs like sparsely sewn wool leggings. My
mom agreed to facial waxing by twelve — I demanded we
do it over summer vacation, so I could try to convince
people that the hair magically vanished when it got hot.
There was shame in having to admit that you had a little
moustache when all the white girls at school didn't even
get wispy hairs on the backs of their thighs. It would be
embarrassing for anyone to call me out on actively trying
for perceived perfection. I had a teacher once describe
white-girl facial hair as "peach fuzz," hair on the cheeks
and above the lip that only shines in the sun. Peach fuzz is
cute! It's pink and soft and you kind of want to rub yourself against it because it feels nice. I've done my research,

MISTER BEAST MAN TO YOU, RANDOR

and there's no positive connotation, at least for a preteen, for "prominent female moustache, subcategory: sable."

So while a man's face near my clitoris was unheard of, the idea was made even worse by the sight of the shorn pussies I saw in pornography, girls that were smooth and rosy, looking more like Hostess treats than real girls. They barely had skin, never mind hair, every inch of them looking the way a woman was supposed to look, like a candy, something you might let roll around in your mouth. I wanted to know how you could get so hairless, so perfect, so determinately female.

My hair came in so thick and unrelenting and widespread that by fourteen my mother was investing in countless implements to make removing it easier: creams that burned the hair clean off but left me with a rash, electric contraptions my older cousins reassured me were virtually painless but actually plucked each hair out individually, and various razors with different benefits — one with built-in moisturizer, one that rotated around your knee without cutting you, one that vibrated to really get at the roots of your hairs. Neeta, the cousin who set up my illicit social media accounts, once sat with me in my mother's bathroom, helping me use a tweezing implement to become as perfectly hairless as she always was. (She brought me a cup of ice and recommended numbing the area first. She was twenty-seven, and I loved running my hand along her tanned, waxed arms.) Regardless, there were only so many hours in the day, and I couldn't dedicate my entire life to eradicating the hair from my face and arms and thighs and calves and back.

At fifteen, I found a thick black hair growing out of my nipple, sticking out like a shard of glass that I somehow never noticed had impaled me. I looked at it all afternoon, trying to decide if it was actually my hair or if a synthetic hairbrush bristle had lodged itself into a part of my body where every sex ed teacher told me it was *physically impossible* to grow hair. None of my female friends reported back from puberty with nipple hair; all they said was that sometimes their periods would hurt and the blood looked more brown than red. My mother never suggested this would happen, either, and her skin was always smooth and poreless. Everything was a lie. It took me a few days before I could bring myself to pluck it; I felt so close to it, like a family member I hated but might possibly grow to love. There's something so carnal about pulling little parts of your body off or out of yourself.

When I did pull the hair out, the root was twice as long as the visible section. I held this iceberg between my fingers, yet another indication from my body saying, "You, you are not quite a woman, inside or out."

Little is worse to a teenage girl – except, maybe, being overweight, or single, or dumped, or not having enough friends, or not getting invited to parties, or not being sexy, or being too sexy, or being a virgin, or not being a

virgin, or being a smartass, or not being smart enough —
than having hair where the world does not think you
should have it. It's rarely you who decides there's something wrong with you; instead, you get your cues from
someone who is the right combination of bored, cruel,
and insecure about themselves to begin with. In the
eighth grade, Junior High Bully and Track Doofus James
sat next to me in English class. Our forearms bumped
and he looked down at my hairy limb, the hair standing
on end from static cling, and compared it to his bald
one. "You're . . . really hairy," he said with the same
wrinkled face you might make if a literal wolf showed
up to class and started rooting around in your backpack. The adult version of me might have retorted with
how much of a shame it was that James's genes were so
weak he couldn't grow any chest hair while I was perfectly capable of growing the full beard of an escaped
convict. But the thirteen-year-old me just squirmed
until I thought enough time had passed for me to pull
my sweater back on.

The white girls I went to school with didn't have sideburns like me, and I never bothered to ask them if they,
too, plucked short, thick, black hairs from the tips of
their noses. (I often heard them talk of "blackheads," and
spent many months considering whether that was white-
girl code for facial hair.) Being a woman, I've always figured, has meant shedding this layer of primal protection.
How is it that evolution still hasn't caught up to me in

knowing that I don't need my anus hair to grow so long that I can braid it?

For me, hair has always meant shame, so imagine my surprise when girls and young women around the world started growing out their armpit hair — easily the worst hair to let go, except, maybe, facial hair — as some feminist aesthetic stance against the patriarchy. Lena Dunham was doing it, Miley Cyrus was doing it (and dyeing it), and it was the movement that launched a thousand online thinkpieces. It was heartening, somewhat, to watch young women take control over their bodies, to give a hearty fuck-you to Big Razor and let their forms be the way men have been permitted to be for centuries.

I considered it, briefly, the same way I consider getting an om tattoo once a year when I happen to drink a thick green juice. It's the kind of feminist statement just subtle enough that you can pretend you're following the status quo, until you wear a tank top and expose your true self: "You thought I was traditionally beautiful, but look at this feminist freak show I turned out to be! I'M GONNA EAT ALL MY BRAAAAS!" But I didn't, the same way I don't cut the hair on my head with much frequency and the same way I maniacally prune the hair on the rest of my body. Hair is a statement, but mine, mine is louder, darker, always less willing to go away. It says too much about me to be affected by mere trends.

How nice it must be to feel so free, so unburdened by the politics of your hair, that you can do whatever you want to it: shave it, cut it, dye it, or just let it exist, worry-free.

It's easier to rebel against hair norms if you're a woman generally unburdened by them in the first place. My hair — brown hair — is politicized in every direction. It's either an unearthly glory, hair so perfect that people want to buy it in bags, or it's an unholy and crude display of the most aggressive kind of femininity: the kind that doesn't actually care about what you consider feminine. When Lena Dunham grows her armpit hair, it's a stance, but not one with much weight. For it to really matter, for your rebellion to extend outside yourself, you have to have been born with hair-baggage — that nagging reminder that what comes out of your body naturally makes you repulsive, or tells people that you're deserving of a slur, or that your sexuality can exist only in a specific vacuum of kink or generous acceptance. Black and brown women know this, in two different ways, but few others do. When Lena grows her body hair out, it's a rebellion. When a brown woman does it, it's a mutiny.

Because, see, I have a great head of hair. I'm prepared to be insecure about almost every part of my body — don't get me started on my *weird veins* — but my hair is perfect. It's long and thick and a perfect mix of rich chocolate brown and magic red lowlights. If I wash it, it's soft and silky. It holds shape. It blow-dries perfectly straight, with a soft flip at the front. I have, in a word, pure-blooded

Indian hair, the kind that other women turn into extensions, bleach into oblivion, and glue onto their scalps. My
hair is perfect, and I know it's perfect because women –
usually white women – ask me how I make it perfect. *Do
you use a particular oil?* they ask. *What about dry shampoo, is
that the secret? Who's your hairdresser? I bet you drink a lot of
coconut water.* I once fell asleep on the bus only to wake
up to a small child petting my head. She told me it was
soft, "like a Barbie's hair," which might have been an
insult but her hands were clean so I let her keep doing it.

But of course, the secret to Indian hair is merely to be
Indian, to have decades of systemic racism, and fear of
the other, and beauty anxiety, and fetishization, and
repulsion woven into your roots. I mean, I use Amla oil
too, but even that is a ploy from Indian cosmetic com-
panies creating products that suggest you, too, could pos-
sess the sheen and strength and length that we got from
our mothers, who got it from their mothers, and so on
and so on. Mostly, it helps to be brown.

Nevertheless, my hair is perfect by a rigid and admittedly colonial standard only. The status quo leads us to
believe thick hair is good, but only on your head, and if
it's light in colour, all the better. We like straight hair –
frizzy or naturally curly hair scares us, namely on a non-
white female body. Scariest of all, maybe, is the hair of
black people, hair so unspeakably different that we think
we are entitled to touch it in public. We scold black
women for letting their natural hair grow out, or we tell

them their braids or twists are "unprofessional" at work. Then we scold them for relaxing their locks or getting weaves, because you can't win unless you were born with the "right" kind of hair. I believe my hair is perfect only because white girls and stupid boys have told me it is perfect. This is my physical worth. I am judged attractive only by what grows out of my head, and only when that is compared to hair we've decided is bad. The price, then, is "unwanted" hair everywhere else on my person.

I cut my hair infrequently. Maybe once every six or eight months. Recently, I cut six inches off and my hair was still long enough to graze my nipples. Regardless, when I saw the hair on the floor of my salon, I felt like Samson, like I had lost the only thing that made me powerful: my one traditionally acceptable beauty marker, gone. It's as if the longer I go, the thicker the hair on my head is, the less white people will notice that the hair on the rest of my body is in a different universe. My "perfect" mane — by someone else's standards, always — means I have an imperfect body, covered in dark fuzz. White girls like to admire how my hair is so silky that it braids without a comb, but rarely do they admire the way my hairline bleeds into my eyebrows, my tiny forehead wolverine-like and swarthy. Other women want my secrets to no split ends (the only answer that's ever pleased them has been, "I don't know, avocado?"), but if I let slip that I shave my entire face multiple times a week, I stop getting invited to parties.

In my grade eight biology class, our teacher gave us a checklist of dominant versus recessive alleles to teach us how babies come out looking the way they do. (The subtext from this particularly nationalistic teacher, clear to me only years later, was that we all end up looking darker and more "vague" than we did in the past. She wasn't exactly unhappy about this, but did express some concern regarding the eventual loss of the blue eye and natural blond.) We were paired up with someone of the opposite sex so we could compare genes to determine what our potential child would look like. Let me really drive this home: a public school teacher in suburban Calgary told her teenage students to pretend they were going to have sex with each other and bear biologically likely babies. I was one of the only ethnic kids in the class. My genes were already steamrolling everyone else's.

My partner, Eric, a white boy who was a Hollister T-shirt personified, went down the genetic checklist with me. When we arrived at "hair on fingers or knuckles," I looked down at my hands for what seemed like the first time. Standing up from the meat of my fingers were soft, black strands of hair. I was horrified. How had I never noticed such a grotesque feature? I always knew my legs were hairy, my arms covered, my upper lip bristled enough to catch flies, but I had overlooked this new barbarity. "Well, I don't have any," Eric said, looking up at me while I hid my hands under the desk. I nodded and said, "Me neither," and we moved on to eye colour – his,

a brilliant green, would be trampled by my molasses sau-
cers, another thing I could not hide. When I got home
that afternoon, I shaved my fingers for the first time, cutting every single knuckle in the process.

I am comfortable with, if not bored by, my hair routines
as an adult. My armpits continue to wage war against
themselves, requiring a shave once a day — more often if
I really want to feel smooth and unblemished. Sometimes
Hamhock will notice little sprouts of hair when I raise
my arms, and will (lovingly, I assume) ask, "Did you shave
today?" A normal person would just answer, but since I
have typically shaved earlier that day and am already
angry at the inevitability of my body, I'll rage against him
and call him weak and make fun of his beard and then
rush to the bathroom to shave, again. Meanwhile, he will
continue cooking, or cleaning, or reading, or doing whatever he was doing before he innocently asked a question
that unpacked my worst instincts about my body. "I was
just asking," he'll say when I return in tears. "I think
you're pretty. I don't know why you don't."

But at least it keeps me busy. I shave my sideburns, my
jawline, and my upper lip so they don't become more
than fuzz. My legs need attention every two days, my
knees a particular hotbed for pin-straight black pricks. I
check my body for stray hairs that don't belong, the way
other women check for moles or lumps or hickeys. And

Brazilian waxes were, for a very long time, a regimented appointment every five weeks. *Here,* I'd say, to a nice blond lady holding a tongue depressor covered in blue wax. *Here is some money for you to put your face close to my vagina, so that I feel more comfortable with someone else doing the same thing for very different reasons.*

I didn't start getting Brazilians until my early twenties. How do you know where to stop with a Brazilian when the rest of your body is covered in hair anyway? Do I just get it waxed like a strawberry blond might, and hope that it doesn't look like I walked into a controlled fire, labia first? Or do I just go for it, really invest, and pour wax over my entire body with the aim of making me as slick and supple as a condom with excellent eyebrows? (That's the other great thing about my hair — it's all over my face and body, but once I separate them, my brows deserve their own illuminated display case.)

My first waxer was May, a talkative flirt who owned a small salon near my apartment, next to a burrito joint. I liked her because she rambled on so much during our waxes that she'd wholly ignore every grunt and squeak and fart that would be squeezed out of my body every time she tore off another strip. "I'm going to Palm Springs!" she'd echo into my vagina, spreading wax on my lips. "It's just me and my girls." Then she'd rip off enough hair to build a plush hamster. I'd make a sound that resembled the air slowly being let out of a balloon, and she'd tell me about the hotel they booked. "It's on the beach and I'm gonna have a mar-ga-riiii-taaaaa!" At least one of us was having fun.

Some women will tell you that waxing is either not as bad as they say, or some kind of necessity if you want to be a sexual creature. Frankly, it's neither. It's a painful procedure that can be mercifully quick with the right person, or dreadfully drawn out. And it's not essential either: the internet and television and movies and the worst influences in your life will tell you that your viability as a sexual object relies solely on your willingness to interact with this exercise in "true" femininity. But those places can also demonstrate how varied womanhood or "femininity" actually is, how little being a woman has to do with what your body does *naturally*. And while I'm not a straight man, I have known enough of them to know that most of them are happy if your vagina doesn't have any teeth.

Many of us women engage in traditional beauty practices for ourselves and ourselves only – my nails are filed sharp and painted bright for no one other than myself, and I wear painful shoes because I like stomping around like a powerful, wobbly giraffe – but plenty of other routines are lines we draw so that other people will consider us beautiful. Which is why it was so heartening to watch women grow out their pit hair, however briefly it lasted. At least they were pushing back against something they just didn't want to do. At least they were having fun, and asking themselves, "Is there one good reason for me to do this? Do I do it for anyone other than the world out-side of my body?" I liked it, even if I couldn't do it.

The day after James pointed out my bushy arms in junior high, I considered adding arm-shaving to my already lengthy list of hair upkeep. Most of my cousins did it, and they were all a decade older and objectively beautiful and lithe and touchable. (I once asked them where they stopped shaving, the arbitrary line that stops you from shearing your entire body. "Well it's not like I have *back hair*," my cousin said as I thought about *all of my back hair*.) Later that week, I ran a razor across a patch of my arm, leaving it frictionless and tanned and soft. That's what was under there? Why didn't anyone tell me? Look at how feminine and delicate I looked! There was hope for me to be beautiful and interesting and worthwhile.

I didn't shave more of it off. I didn't want James to know he had gotten to me, so I figured I'd wait until the summer, the way I did for my moustache and brows, so that everyone would just forget I ever had hair in the first place. In class, though, James noticed the bald patch on my forearm. He laughed. "Did you try shaving your arm because I told you that you were hairy?"

James works in finance now. He lives in Boston. We are all eventually punished for our sins.

I still shave my knuckles, a decade after first noti-cing the hair. I've mastered the art of tugging a razor across the meaty part of my finger, never going over it twice to avoid razor burn. I don't cut myself as often as I used to. Maintaining this insecurity gets easier with every passing year. The hair never stops coming back, it never slows down, it never listens to me. It's a quintessential encapsulation of running after an unattainable goal: we turned this basic fact about our bodies into something ugly.

I often wonder while I'm in the shower, running my razor across my fingers even if I don't actually see any hair, what it is I'm trying to prove and to whom. That I'm a woman, a real, live woman with a Frequent Waxer card at Aroma Spa? That if I leave the house with knees that prickle, I'll run into James, his still-hairless face grinning at me about how stupid I am for trying to pretend to be someone that I so clearly am not? He'll tell me that I'm ugly, that I'm not worthy of being out in the sun, that I don't deserve love or to be in the presence of a white boy like him, one who might like me even if I let my sideburns grow down my face.

Then I'll cut myself, right on the joint, and the water swirling into the tub's drain will run red.

At our last appointment, May welcomed me the way she always did, by mispronouncing my name ("Sketchy!") and motioning me into a free room. I disrobed, briefly fretting about whatever scents or emulsions were coming from my body, before resigning myself to the fact that it was too late. She told me to lie down and leaned into me to examine her workspace, an overgrown garden she needed to hack at to make a delicate triangle or a heart or a sexy Hitler moustache.

"I'm going to Vegas with some of my girls in a few weeks!" she said, starting with the first strip. She ripped off sheet after sheet, and I only got a brief glimpse at what came off: my black hairs caught in golden wax, like bugs frozen in blocks of amber.

She was halfway through making me an acceptable woman, telling me about the suite she and her girlfriends would be renting, when she stopped midsentence. Her eyes glazed over and her breathing grew shallow. For a second, I thought she had ripped my clitoris clean off my body and I was too numbed to this process to even notice. "Are you okay?" I asked, propping myself up to look at her. I was bare from the waist down, a flap of wax paper still stuck to my body. With her right hand, she clutched her chest, and with the other, she levelled herself – by putting her hand down on my vagina. "I can't breathe," she said. "Just give me a second." *Of course*, I thought. *How could I leave you in a moment like this? You're having chest pains and I'm not wearing any pants.*

May politely excused herself (as politely as one can when having a medical emergency while a second party is naked on a table). Another woman came in to finish the job, and I left the salon $50 poorer and pretty sure that my hair had finally, unbelievably, killed someone.

When I hold Raisin – she is still small enough to hold, for now – she brushes my hair with her fingers. When she was even younger, she'd sit in my lap and pull my long hair over my face and yell, "I see you!" Younger than that still, I'd wave locks of my hair over her face while she was lying on a baby blanket, and she'd laugh and coo and try to pull it to her mouth. Now, she tells me things like, "Boo, your hair is too long, it's getting all over me." Hers is wild and curly and unmanageable, remarkably different from that of anyone on our side of the family. Her eyebrows are bold and will become thick like mine. I'm noticing soft light-brown hairs on her back that are darker each time I see her. I don't know if she's noticed. Raisin is at that perfect age when she isn't occupied with her own beauty because no one has yet told her to be. She hates it when you brush her hair; she likes it in a low ponytail, maybe tucked under a Blue Jays cap. I wonder if she'll get our knuckle hair, our pubescent moustaches, our hairy toes and necks. I wonder if she'll wish she had hair like mine, thick and long and black and ideal, while also thankful she didn't get my arm hair, forehead hair, chin hair. Or maybe she will, and she'll be thankful all the same.

After possibly murdering my waxer – it was, apparently, your garden variety panic attack and nothing more – I didn't go back for a wax, any wax, for a few months. I gave my body a break; I let my hair grow wild and curl around me and build a protective cocoon of

Papa <papa@gmail.com>, April 11, 2012

You're coming home tomorrow. Well, we have to find the good in everything, I suppose.

Tawi River, Elbow River

——

My parents still live in the same house I grew up in, an unremarkable four-bedroom, two-and-a-half-bath cookie cutter that looks like every other house in the neighbourhood except for its peach exterior. I don't think they had any say in the house being pinkish rather than grey or blue, but something feels perfect about ours being a little too cartoonish for the area. There's a porch and front yard that's always manicured but never used and a backyard that was scattered with sour fruit from an apple tree every fall until the tree started rotting and had to be cut down. Our block is deeply suburban, the only edge being the outpatient treatment centre located across the street in the middle of a massive park. The patients are quiet, most of the time, though sometimes teenagers are seen running away from the compound, with an adult bolting after them. Once I found a cigarette butt on the sidewalk in front of our driveway. It was very exciting.

I had birthdays in the living room, temper tantrums in my bedroom, and friends over to roller skate in our unfinished concrete basement. When my brother got married we had three of the four ceremonies in our family room and backyard. My mom fainted next to the television one morning when she skipped breakfast, and five years later, in the same spot, I told her and my dad that I got into a university that was on the other side of the country. My niece, Raisin, was born almost two years later, and three years after that, as we played in my mother's closet with her heaviest gold jewellery, Raisin looked at me with her big blue bulb eyes and said, for the first time, "Oh, Boo, I love you!" – a sentence I am not sure she understood at the time, but one that has bound me to her ever since.

When I have nightmares, ones where my parents die and I am devastated and I can't fathom standing straight, I image scenarios where my brother and I have to decide what to do with the house. Do we sell it, hoping another family takes over the four bedrooms, finally making use of the Jacuzzi my mother filled with plants and decorative soaps? Maybe someone will rip up the remaining carpet, getting rid of the big black stain in my bedroom where I dropped an eyeliner brush. Maybe they'll finally finish the basement.

I already know I don't want to get rid of the house. My parents don't need the space and, eventually, they won't want the stairs, the stand-up shower, the echoing foyer, but I want them to live there forever. This house has always been my home, even when I hated it and wanted to leave. But I keep forgetting that for my dad in particular it's a far cry from the place he remembers the most as being home.

The home we grew up in was a big get for my parents, proof that they'd succeeded in achieving the immigrant dream, so of course they filled it with memories of another home. Next to the front door is a stitched wall hanging of Ganesh, little mirrors sewn onto his arms and belly. The front room has coffee-table books with photos of Kashmir and Jammu. In the kitchen, my dad has put up a black-and-white photo of his mother and father standing expressionless next to each other in a barren room, my grandfather wearing those same thick-rimmed black glasses he wears in every other photo I've seen of him, and my grandmother in a white sari draped over her head.

My dad has a well-trodden pattern in this house: he wakes up at seven and runs five or ten kilometres (I say *kil-aw-metres* and he says *kill-o-metres* and then we mock each other's accents, his still faintly Indian or British and mine Albertan and drawling) and has a breakfast of grapefruit or melon and a handful of soaked almonds. ("It makes the fibre easier to digest," he says, dropping exactly ten on your plate without asking you.) Then he'll settle in his armchair, the leather one in the corner of the family room, the one next to the wooden folding table shaped like a flower (I think we got that in India too) where he keeps the remotes. The phone is next to him too, usually. By ten-thirty he's reclining. This is where he watches television, for hours, or falls asleep with the sun on his face from the big living room window facing the backyard. In his bedroom, later, he does yoga, flipping himself upside down and muttering to himself about how his joints aren't what they used to be. This is Papa's house, and the only time his comfortable routine is interrupted is when Raisin sleeps over. She insists on sleeping in their bed with my mom, and kicks him out before he can even climb in. So he sleeps in the guest bedroom, the one his mother once used.

My grandmother moved from India to live with us for a few years, and the house smelled like mothballs while she was forever watching *Days of Our Lives*. (She spoke no English, but could somehow tell you exactly what was happening to Marlena that week.) But she hated it at our house in Canada. Everything was too cold and too foreign. She moved back to India to live with my dad's younger brother, my Chacha, who lived in the same house that nearly everyone in my family has lived in at some point.

It's easy for me to forget that my dad used to live somewhere else, somewhere too far away to imagine: a house on a sprawling property in what was then rural India, that would later be on the other side of a string of fruit markets, spice shops, and a man who sold cutesy notebooks and pens with British colloquialisms on them. When we visited India when I was ten, we stayed in this old house, though it had been taken over by his little brother, his sister-in-law, and their two kids. My grandmother still lived there too, and when my brother flew in a few weeks later, there were ten of us staying in that house. My cousins shared a room with our grandmother, my brother and I slept in the master bedroom with my parents, and my aunt and uncle slept in the living room.

The house and front yard were encircled by a black fence with a gate too heavy for me to close properly. Once, I accidentally let a cow into the property, and Chacha watched it eat the single flower he had been able to grow in the yard. When I giggled, he threatened to feed me to the cow. Every morning, a man would knock on the gate with his cane and speak in lyrical Hindi, and my aunt would tell me to take a coin from a bucket in the living room and toss it into his bucket. He had a long beard and carried a staff, and when the coin plunked into his bucket, he stopped speaking, nodded, and moved on.

My memories of India are sparse but vivid, such as how I couldn't speak to the other kids who didn't know any English, so instead I acted like a dog to make them

The second story is about the night he died, on his roof, while my grandmother was changing my brother's diaper.

I can't remember what I'm supposed to call my grandfather because I have never had to call him – I was born nearly twelve years after his death. I became my family's new roots, digging deep into a Canadian culture that loved beef, farming, whiteness – the opposite of what my family knew.

We returned to the house recently. In the time since our last family trip to Jammu, more than ten years earlier, the last of my grandparents had died, my cousins had gotten married, my brother had married and they'd had Raisin. I don't know if anyone else wanted to see the house, but it was the only place I felt I remembered or felt connected to. Everything else in India feels so separate from me – I wasn't born there, I never lived there, I don't understand what anyone is saying, but I remember the house. Besides, Chacha was trying to sell it, so it felt important to visit it for what would likely be the last time.

In my memory, the old house was bright pink, a more saturated colour than our house in Calgary, with the windows always flung open, the door as wide as I was tall. I remember the path that ran from the black front gate to the entrance was a mile long, and the high ceilings, and the green acre of land they had for a backyard.

As we walked down an unlit alleyway to the house at dusk, nothing looked familiar. Mom walked next to me, watching my face instead of watching the road (which is dangerous if you're averse to stepping in actual bullshit). She was waiting for my expression to light up at the familiar sight of a fence or an awning or a window, but nothing connected. Mom's pace slowed as we approached a black fence that I remembered being on the other side of the road. And wasn't the entrance right on the corner? And wasn't the gate big enough to let a car in and not, say, a well-fed toddler?

"This is it?" I asked Mom.

"Well, what else?"

The house wasn't salmon pink like it used to be. Instead, it was a grey, dusty rose. It was smaller than I remembered, too, but then everything is when you return to something you knew when you were much smaller yourself. Ivy was growing all over the side, and the renters had put up a sign promoting the computer classes they hosted there, something Chacha permitted for free until he can sell the property. The grass looked grey too, though admittedly, it had been a chilly winter. The front door was padlocked shut. The side door that my cousin and I would bolt out of to run up the stairs to the roof was locked too, and so narrow that I didn't know how I ever fit through it.

My dad's cousin walked around to the side door and asked me to shine the flashlight from my phone onto the lock so he could find the right key. When he unlocked it, the door stuck until he wrenched it open, and then he waited for me to walk in. I had to tilt my body sideways to enter.

The kitchen table took up more of the front room than I remembered. The master bedroom and living room were filled with little desks and old computers. The windows were boarded up. The light was dim and yellow, the way it always was at night because of rolling brownouts that everyone in the country seemed used to. Raisin ran between rooms, touching everything in the exact way we had all expressly told her not to because her hand inevitably ends up wedged inside her mouth seconds later.

We stood in the middle of the house and took up more room than I thought we should. "This is smaller than I remember," I told my dad, and he laughed. "See the ceiling fans?" he said, pointing up. "We used to just have the one for the longest time. Even in the summer." The ceiling was peeling now, the fans broken, and all the bedroom doors were locked. My father's cousin went around opening the doors, all except the one to my grandmother's old bedroom. He said he didn't have the key for that one. My cousins had shared this room with Behenji, so the door was covered with stickers of Daffy Duck, their own drawings of cartoon Hindu deities, and clippings from children's magazines. On another door was a drawing of Ganesh, apparently done by my cousin and me. Our names were written at the bottom of the picture, but I don't remember doing it, or know why Chacha would have kept it on a door in the house for a decade.

My dad pulled a stool away from next to the fridge (squat, small, still as small as I remembered) and sat while we all stood. He looked at the kitchen door and then leaned back with his hands wrapped around one knee. "In the summers, we would take a few bottles, jerry cans, and go to the canal outside," he said. "Did you notice, it's like a sewer? It used to be a beautiful canal where I learned swimming."

"It was gushing water," Mom added.

"Wonderful water, and it was ice cold. We'd go, dip the jerry cans in that. We'd have ourselves a little meal and we'd have cold water. It was bucolic!" He talked about mango season, about how his dad built this house. I walked around the house again, alone, while my mom told my sister-in-law the story of how my brother pulled a pot of boiling oil onto himself as a toddler, his skin blistering but somehow leaving only a minuscule scar on his leg as an adult. ("I thought Chacha was going to kill me," Mom said, because her priorities are bad.)

I took the stairs to the roof and wondered who would let their children run up and down such narrow and crooked and curved stairs with no railing, unsupervised. The rooms upstairs were open but empty, just as they were when I last visited. The view was different too: countless new homes had been built, meaning more clotheslines, more distant echoes of children yelling. Fewer cows.

Raisin called for me at the foot of the stairs: "Boo, where did you go?" I didn't want her on those deathstairs without help, so I went back down.

When we got back to the main area, Papa was speaking, largely to himself, about maybe keeping the property and renovating it. "I could come here in the winters. All it really needs is some fresh paint. Or, well, not really, we'd have to build the whole place up again." My mother and I shared a furtive glance because this is something he says every few months, anytime something reminds him of home: *Maybe we should move to India?* Plenty of the baby-boomer men in my family have said this: hit sixty and decided it was time to return to a place they left thirty, forty years ago. They never follow through, though, because what they're missing isn't the place, the way the sun hits the palm tree outside your window, the way that hot weather always makes the air look reddish, even at night. What they miss are people who are long gone, a version of their lives where they were ten and dipping jerry cans into a canal, and brothers and sisters still lived together in the same house without children, needy goddamn children who don't speak Hindi or Kashmiri and don't even know what a kitab is when you threaten to hit them with one. Old world, yes. So old it's unattainable. I suspect that even our relatives who stay in India miss this too.

My dad hated India and he always wanted to leave. Whenever we visit, he throws little fits about cleanliness of towels, or cockroaches found dead in corners. "How did he survive here?" I asked my mom during one spritely fit about the way the towels at our hotel were folded.

"Why do you think he left?"

By all standards, my father's new home in Canada and my uncle's new home in India are "better." Papa's house is bigger, heated consistently, and we have had only two blackouts that I can remember due to weather and not common circumstances. I got my first computer at twelve and the internet was lightning fast. Indians who move to North America chirp, "Better life, a better life!!!!" nearly constantly at their children, largely when their westernized asshole children misbehave.

But the only way to do better, to have better, is to lose pieces of what was. It's inevitable that you can't bring everything with you, like carrying water in your cupped hands from one river to another. There are too many cracks, and if you're so eager to move, you'll just have to get used to new water.

The third story I have about my grandfather I heard while we were standing in the main room next to the sink at Chacha's old house where we used to brush our teeth and wash our hands. My dad sighed heavily and pointed at the mirror hanging over the sink. "I can still see my dad, sitting in front of that mirror and shaving." His voice cracked and he rubbed his eyes. "My mother would be across, over here in the kitchen cooking. And he would sit on a little daybed and I would watch him shave."

He coughed and rested the weight of his head on two fingers. "I should keep that mirror."

Since Papa returned home to Calgary—his second home, I guess—he's taken a step back from wanting to keep the house he grew up in. "If I went to the house, there's nobody," he said. "The purpose of going into a comfortable cocoon defeats itself. It seems that when you reach a certain stage in life, you revert back to something more familiar, something more familial. I can't explain it to you," Papa said. "It just happens."

My parents have renovated their home significantly in the past decade: hardwood flooring, a completely new kitchen, fresh coats of paint. All our toilets used to be rectangular for some reason, something I felt a perverted sense of pride in because it was so weird. They got new ones, oval ones, which is boring and kind of depressing, and they feel a little too high for a house filled with short bodies. Mom has reorganized the kitchen so that now the one room that was everyone's room is foreign to me. My visits are punctuated with me whipping around, angrily demanding, "Where are the forks, WHY DID YOU MOVE THE FORKS?" and she has to calmly open the drawer on the other side of the kitchen as if she moved it just to ruin my life. I just found out where she put the bowls and their new location feels like such a personal attack that I can barely talk about it without raising my blood pressure.

But at least my parents still live there, so our routines get to be the same. Mom comes into my room — which now has a very large forgery of *The Creation of Adam* for no reason whatsoever — and tells me I'm messy and starts trying to clean before I have to yell at her to leave. At night, she lets me lie down on the couch with my head in her lap and she strokes my hair for hours until bedtime. It's the same home I knew as a kid, but, frankly, better. Like all things you leave but can't forget, it somehow gets warmer, sepia-toned, and unattainable in your memory.

My parents' childhoods sound impossible to me. Everything is about open expanses of land, running around with sticks and playing with rocks. Mom sounded like a tyrant and Papa sounded hungry all the time. They didn't even like me playing in the front yard without intense supervision. I've exoticized everything about their old homes, and I think they have too. It's been so long, it's so far now, the only thing you can do is remember it as perfect. Mom hasn't returned to her childhood home in Srinagar for thirty-plus years, but she talks about it with such melancholy, such a sense of loss that I feel it too. I do this too now, like when I talk about Mom's cooking (I refuse to eat any other Indian food) or when I think about how I figured out how to crack the window open far enough so I could sit on the roof at two in the morning. When I can't sleep, I think about how reassuring it was to hear my parents watching David Letterman on the little television in the room next to mine, how in the morning I could hear their bare feet sink into the white carpet.

Rhythms of the house have changed since Raisin took over. She wants to jump on all the beds and eat whipped cream straight from the freezer and use her baseball bat in the house. When she sleeps over, she sleeps in my old room, which used to be my brother's room, or in her grandparents' bed, another place I feel like I still own. My dad's armchair isn't his anymore; she sprawls across it instead and refuses to leave. She's taken his seat at the kitchen table, too. And his aluminum water bottle. And his office, now filled with plastic baseball bats and Disney tea sets and board games. "Do I own anything in here?" Papa once muttered to himself, and Raisin replied with, "NO, IT'S MINE."

When I visit home, then, I live out of a suitcase, and, since the house hardly looks the same, I listen for sounds that remind me that this is home. Mom closes the glass door of her shower: that is morning. Papa flicks on the radio: that is early afternoon. His armchair creaks and snaps to bring up the leg rest: that's late afternoon. A pressure cooker screams in the kitchen: it's almost dinnertime. The curtains are closed in the living room and it sounds like soft strips of fabric are being gently torn: my parents are going to bed. My apartment doesn't have these same sounds; instead, my sounds are a cat pawing through her food bowl, the front door being locked, the swish of sheets being readjusted. These sounds don't feel the same. They don't feel as comforting, because they are mine, are my responsibility, while the ones at home are my parents' — the promise that everything is fine, consistent, safe at home.

—

Chacha's new house is far from the home he grew up in with my father, in a more suburban area I'd never been to before. It's comparatively palatial, all marble and bright flowers in the yard and a porch swing. Raisin and I went for the swing as soon as we saw it. "Your grand-mother liked that seat too," Chacha told me. They have a computer, a desktop that isn't very fast but gets the job done. All the bedrooms have big windows that let in plenty of light.

On one side of the house is a dirt road that leads back to the city, and on the other, a few miles away, is Pakistan. The internet conked out a lot, and I asked my uncle why that kept happening. For a country booming with indus-try and at the very tip of the IT industry, it's a weird prob-lem to have. He rifled through a junk drawer and pulled out a little lead slug.

"What do you think this is?" he asked me.

I weighed it in my hand. "A bullet?"

"It flew from the Pakistani border to our house and landed on the roof. And that's why the internet is so slow here."

There is always unrest around here – the airport is a military airport, and Jammu's connection with Kashmir means you see men in green berets with rifles walking around, smoking skinny cigarettes – but you wouldn't know it by the evenings we spent at Chacha's house.

Guava grows in the backyard, and it is bright pink and so sweet that I didn't even bother dusting it with salt like I had been taught by my mother, the way to tolerate Canadian amrood. Everything here is pink and cozy. My brother and I didn't want to leave. We had no interest in travelling, in visiting attractions. We just liked being home.

This was nothing like the house I remember my uncle having, but it might be closer to what he and my dad remember. There isn't a ravine, but a goat walked past our window followed by a little boy trying to guide him in the right direction. If that isn't bucolic, nothing is.

My brother, sister-in-law, Raisin, and I left India two weeks before my parents. Chacha helped us pack our bags into his car before driving us to the airport. Mom and Papa hugged us goodbye – none of us cried, largely because I think we had all had enough of each other for a few weeks at least. Chachi cried so hard that I wanted her to go back inside. "You'll come back, haan?" she asked me. I told her of course, but she kept crying, and hugged me one more time before pushing me away from her.

When we climbed into the car, I turned back for one last look at this new house, at the new gate in freshly painted black, and at the plate affixed to the fence with the house's address. Above the house number is "Prithvi," my grandfather's name, one last link to a man who will never see this house or the people in it. We drove off to the airport, and I watched as his name shrank in the distance.

from a warring religion, never mind sneaking out to a heavily wooded area in our suburb so we could lie in the sun together.

To get to the park, you had to walk through a puddled alley to a small forest, with tall trees that obscured the sky, thick brush that made it impossible to see the end of the path until you caught a glimpse of a little slide. We'd hide behind the bushes next to the park while younger girls crawled on the jungle gym and tried to complete a full loop on the swings.

My boyfriend wanted us to keep the park, or more pressingly, our relationship, a secret, and I never asked for anything different. We already knew it was impossible, we would never make it out alive if our parents found out. He once invited me over to his house when his parents were away and he showed me around and said, "Do you like it?" It was important that I did because we probably wouldn't be in each other's homes again. He guided me into his family's kitchen and I thought to myself, *This will never last.* Once, before I even met my brown boyfriend, a white boy in my high school asked me on MSN instant messenger to be his girlfriend. I said okay mostly because saying no seemed rude, and besides, he was on the football team, he had shiny teeth and blue eyes, dimples in both cheeks. Who was I to say no to an interested boy, like some *caucasian.* His name was white, forgettable, something that even now makes me think of warm, soggy bread, or crackers with the salt brushed off. He'd ask me on dates, to the mall, to the movies, places where people – my people – might see us, and never understood my suggestions: "How about you go into the theatre first and I'll sneak in after. You'll know me by the wool face-mask I'll be wearing. Very trendy for spring." So it was comforting that this real boyfriend and I had an unspoken agreement, and that he never deigned to ask me to the movies.

We only told a few people that we were dating, but word spread regardless, so we were paranoid someone would tell one of our cousins would tell our uncle would tell our moms. My mom did, indeed, find out – she claimed an aunty drove past the park where we spent our Saturdays – and demanded that I break it off, lest I be disowned. This was a real threat, one that shook me up because, while it was calamitous that Mom knew, it would be a literal life-ender if Papa did. I told my mother I would dump the boy to stay out of trouble, but I didn't: we just learned to be better liars, to be quieter, to take our feelings and squeeze them until they were unperceivable to anyone other than us. It was worth it to lie, even though we knew it was temporary. Our choices were always between family and freedom. Neither, frankly, were all that easy to walk away from. But it didn't matter much: we broke up right before I moved out of my hometown for university. We met up in the park for the last time and said goodbye. "It was never going to work," he told me. I nodded and cried and we hugged while small children climbed the jungle gym near us, beyond the pine.

That relationship was all about restrictions, about working within the confines we needed to in high school. We didn't want to get in trouble, to have our morality questioned by the cultural norms within our families. We didn't want a fight, to lose the protective wing of a brown mother, and we knew we each understood this. When it was too risky, he never pressed me to come out anyway, to sneak around when our parents were suspicious.

Hamhock was never like this. When we started dating, I refused to tell my friends about him, to bring him up with my cousins, to acknowledge him anywhere other than in my own head. I figured he would be temporary, a future joke between my friends and me, like, "Remember that Lego-shaped guy you dated for three weeks?" But every date or interaction with him felt like sinking into warm quicksand. He invited me over to his apartment, a two-bedroom on the other side of town, and he made me lobster. He taught me how to crack its claws open, suck meat out of its joints, break its back and dip it into burgundy ramekins filled with melted butter. He met me at the ferry docks and held my hand – pinky between his index and ring fingers, for some reason – while we sailed to the beach, where he would let me hang off his back in the water, the only kind of swimming I like. Once, I made a passing joke about an old shelf in his bathroom, the white paint chipping off and gathering in little corners or flaking off onto my fingers. The next weekend when I came over, he had sanded it down, painted it anew in ghost white. I ran my hand across it and knew, for sure, this was serious.

Hamhock first told me he loved me two weeks into dating. I was in Toronto, folding laundry at eleven in the morning, and he was tailgating a football game in Buffalo. He called me, clearly a few drinks deep, from a porta-potty. "I love you!" he said, and the rest was incoherent before he hung up on me. I continued to date him after that, possibly because I had low self-esteem but more realistically because he felt like home. "Falling in love" sounds so passive, but it did feel unintentional, like tripping into a pit that happened to be filled with downy gold.

So it was early in the genesis of our relationship when Hamhock asked me why my parents didn't know about him. Without hesitation, he had taken me home and shown me off to his parents and extended family, and everyone seemed relieved that he had found someone as intolerable as him. But my parents didn't know, my cousins didn't ask, I didn't bring him home with me for years. He wanted to be real, to be acknowledged. My first boyfriend and I understood the necessity of being secretive, but to Hamhock, it felt like shame.

I don't like change, or making big decisions. I don't like changing my personal status quo even when my status quo isn't comfortable. For Hamhock, it was easy: you just call up your folks and tell them you're in *looove*, that it's so *cooosmic*, maybe adding some nonsense about how this is the *ooone* — platitudes that, overwhelmingly, brown families are immune to. "The *one*?" I imagined my father saying. "What the hell are you talking about? Five years ago, you were crying about Orlando Bloom marrying some waif with two different eye colours but now, *this is the one*." I pictured my mother, meanwhile, weeping endlessly, throwing herself on fainting couches — any couch you faint on is a fainting couch if you just *believe* — and threatening to die, to just drop dead right there because of her daughter's rebellion.

I tried explaining to Hamhock that our age difference — an impressive thirteen years — would be the greatest issue. When I told my brother about him — my brother who is twelve years older than me — at first he took Hamhock's side. "They'll get over it," he said. "You're an adult, they'll make their peace with it. You know they can't hold grudges."

"He's thirteen years older than I am," I told him.

My brother let out a heavy sigh, punctuated at the end by a mournful "aaauuughhhhhhhhh." He mumbled to himself for a moment. "Yeeeaaah," he said. "That's not going to work."

My brother knew, as I knew, that this would be an uphill battle, a lifelong standoff until either I or my parents died. (I am, still, not convinced they won't outlive me, like lovable radioactive cockroaches or crushing personal debt.) Hamhock was white, which wasn't necessarily a problem but hardly ideal. He was older than the surface of the earth, adding to a poorly imagined narrative of me, an innocent, being subverted by an old man.

But the biggest barrier, ultimately, had nothing to do with Hamhock and everything to do with my genetics: I'm a girl, and brown girls are inevitably treated differently than their brothers or male cousins. My brother married a white girl and moved in with her before marriage to limited if only muted controversy. For me, however, the baby in the family, the least willing to "behave" and, worse, a *girl*, the rules are rewritten and rarely in my favour. It wasn't fair, but it was predictable.

When I was twelve or thirteen and starting to notice boys and they were noticing me (but more like how you "notice" a pelican is eating your lunch on the beach), I thought about what it might take to get my dad's approval to date someone. A white boy, of course, in part because there were so few brown guys around, but mostly so that I could have the ultimate approval of being loved by a white boy. (Getting male attention was one thing; getting white male attention meant something even better, at least to my woefully under-developed brain.) The guy maybe wouldn't like me at first, but through some disaster, some unknowable misfortune, we'd find each other. Our classroom would have to burst into flames and he'd have to save me, or maybe a school shooter would take over the entire building and I would guide him to safety in the vents. Or what about me getting a horrible illness? A boy could nurse me back to health after a bout of vein cancer, or maybe he could help me see the value of life after a severe thrombosis scare, a disease I had only heard of once and knew absolutely nothing about. That, I figured, would be enough to convince my parents that it was okay to let me date, that it would be good for me, that they would approve of this deviation in my life. The worst thing that ever happened to me as a teenager, apparently, was not being drastically and irrevocably ill.

Hamhock wouldn't come to my parents like this, like a saviour, like a salve. Our story was delightful in its mundanity: we met, it worked, we're trying. So after my brother's reaction I did nothing, told no one else in my family. It's hard to encapsulate years of your partner quietly waiting for you to take action, of them sitting next to you and though they hold their tongue about the brown elephants in the room, you can hear the constant buzzy hum of them wanting more from you.

Few things get less complicated as you age, but your family, that at least should become easier. You should eventually make peace with everyone, with their decisions and their quirks. With your parents in particular, you should fight less because you have less time to fight. But when I finally did build up the courage to tell my parents about Hamhock, years into dating, I felt that memorable sting of something being so deeply not easy. Over the phone, while my mother said, "I will write in my blood that I will never speak to you again," and my father told me, "When I have a stroke, you will remember this," I thought to myself, *This is exactly as hard as I thought it would be.*

Mom begged me to break up with him. "Just end it," she told me, steeling her voice to emphasize the demand for finality, for her command to be obeyed. And so I did the same thing I had done as a teenager: "Okay," I told her the next day. "I did. We're done." Her breathing eased and she was friendly again, her anger washed away by my simple act of lying, again, this time a wildly unlivable lie. Hamhock knew I'd lied and he shrank into himself a little more, and the buzz of him hoping for more got louder. Besides that, I was angry for acquiescing – four years living across the country from my parents, an adult old enough to, say, legally purchase a pack of cigarettes and swallow them whole if I wanted, and I was still lying to my mother about who I was dating just to prevent a fight.

Later that week, I confessed to her we were still dating. "I don't know why you're doing this to me," she said, perhaps fanning herself while wearing a feather boa-trimmed robe, mascara running down her face. "Just bring him home and let us meet him." Mom was flexing towards acceptance, theatrically, like shattering a window to get inside a house when the door is unlocked.

"I think they'll like me," Hamhock said, because he is always sweet, so sweet, and so stupid. We spent a year trying to find the right reason to go home, a good excuse that felt organic and as normal as possible when you're bringing a boy home to disapproving parents. A friend from high school was getting married and I was in her bridal party, so what better time than her wedding to bring him home? (It's this, I thought, or a funeral, and there's rarely cake at funerals.) Hamhock assumed approval would come merely from meeting him, that he just needed to see my mom in person, but she wasn't the one I was worried about. Mom is unwilling to fight for long. The older she gets, the weaker her rage, the less willing she is to protest the inevitable. But Papa has become more solid, more irritable, less willing to cooperate. Papa is still, at sixty-six, a lot of work. When I first told them about Hamhock, Mom had her moment of vocal panic, but Papa didn't talk to me for three months.

"It's not about them liking you," I said. "It's about him accepting you."

Papa is difficult, and this either charming character quirk or destructive force of nature is on display best in the first half-hour when I visit home. My mother is always the one to greet me at the airport. My father, meanwhile, usually idles in their Ford Escape in the arrivals lot and waits for me to come to him. He gives me a big hug and a kiss on the cheek, his beard rubbing against my skin and giving me a synesthesia-like tingle in my brain. "Hellllllo," he'll say before trying to lift my bag into the trunk and then getting upset that my bag is so heavy and why did I need to pack this much before I end up taking over loading the bag and say that I never asked him to pick up my bag and I am perfectly content with what I brought and maybe lay off a second. "How was the flight?" he'll ask. Then he'll tell me exactly how many minutes ahead or behind I am. If I'm right on time, he'll marvel at it while we pull away from the airport. "Not even a minute off schedule!" he'll holler. "Amazing. Would you believe it?" I tell him that yes, I can, because that is how planes work.

In the first few minutes of these drives, I am my cleverest to him, while he's at his most charming. I can forgive his garbled pronunciations – like the time he saw a sign saying "Pet-Co" and read it aloud as "Pedophile" – and he can forgive my insistence on being the smartest guy in the room, like that one drive home where I baited him into a conversation about sexual assault statistics just so that I could be right about something. Once, we drove past a church offering a free lunch, and he tried to persuade my mother and me to pretend being Christians just to get a sandwich. "Could save me a few bucks," he said, chuckling and accidentally speeding past a traffic cop.

But the drive from the Calgary International Airport to my childhood home in a dead-silent neighbourhood sandwiched between gas stations lasts around half an hour. It's just long enough that by the time we're pulling into the garage, my father has already found fault with how much clavicle I have dared show in his presence and I am already irritated by the way I think he looked at my thigh, indicating that he thinks it's too big.

My trips last anywhere from four days to ten, and the tone we establish in that car ride is then set for the rest of my visit. His refusal to learn correct terminology stops being cute and starts being grating. "It's not *Jazzy*," I'll say. "It's Jay-Z. And his wife is not named *Shobna* or *Binaka*. You have the internet, how is this happening?" And he will stop finding my willfulness, my stubborn attitude, endearing and will start finding it an impetus to peaceful coexistance. "Just because you went to Paris for five days, once, three years ago, does not mean you know more about wine than me," he will say, unscrewing a bottle of sour white and refusing to give me any. Then we fight. We'll have an argument where I call him selfish and he calls me ungrateful, and by nightfall of day one, we're not speaking. Without fail, we spend 70 per cent of the visit giving each other a staunch silent treatment, icing each other out in a way typically reserved for mortal enemies forced to attend the same office potluck.

It was a version of this scene that I anticipated before my flight to Calgary to introduce Hamhock to my family. I went a few days ahead. As usual, Papa drove my mom to the airport, but he didn't get out of the car to greet me. He didn't chat much in the car either, didn't say something about "the inescapable darkness of human existence" or ask me about "that girl you met when you first moved to Toronto, what's her name, Gibbon or something?" Instead, when we got home, he just roamed around the house in his slippers, looking down, readjusting picture frames that didn't need adjusting.

"So," he tried once. "Does he . . . What does he . . . Is he tall?"

"No," I said, "he's not tall." Papa nodded.

When Hamhock landed, my mom, Raisin, and I picked him up from the airport. Raisin ran at him for a hug and he sat in the back of the car with her, feeding her little doughnuts. He called my mom Mrs. Koul, as I'd suggested. When we got home, Papa was still pacing in the foyer.

They shook hands. Papa led him into the kitchen, where all serious family matters tend to take place. He offered Hamhock tea. "You look good," Papa said. "For someone your age." It was . . . fine. It was *fine*. Hamhock listened to my advice and accepted three helpings of food from my mother, even when full. He played with Raisin, who seemed to want to sit directly on his head whenever he was around, asking to play on his phone or to talk to her about baseball. He joined my brother in his favourite activity: staunch, cranky silence while staring at a *Seinfeld* rerun.

There wasn't a fight until four days in, when Hamhock went rogue and suggested to my parents that he and I move in together. Papa's face, which had otherwise been locked in a lightly clenched aspect, filled with all his blood like it always does when he's furious. He told Hamhock it was impossible, it would never happen, that no one in the family had ever lived with a

SCAACHI KOUL

partner out of wedlock. (This was hardly the truth. Papa was lying either out of intentional misdirection or because of a blocked-out memory – my brother and his wife, for one, moved in together after four months of dating.) Hamhock nodded respectfully. "I wouldn't want to do anything to upset you," he told my dad, while I stormed off upstairs to lock myself in my room, cry in my pillow, and maybe let out one tortured scream of, "BUT IT'S NOT FAAAAAAAAAAAAAAAIIIIIIRRRRR." Just one of the classics.

At one point during the week, Papa told Hamhock he was "bothered" by how much he liked him, as if digging down into his disapproval would have been easier if Hamhock were the monster he'd invented in his head. We left Calgary emotionally exhausted, our bellies aching from too much rogan josh and raita. Back at his apartment, which was starting to feel too small for both of us to sit in, we unpacked the trip. I knew Hamhock had been hoping for some immediate reversal, as if meeting him would make my dad say, "Why, he's perfect! Take my daughter, please! My decades of cultural stipulations and moral repudiations have vanished merely by seeing your powerful haunches and formidable calves!"

Instead, we talked about what to do with, at best, my father tuning out a relationship he might have preferred to occur behind his back, and at worst, his explicit disapproval of our going forward with it in a more meaningful way.

"What now?" Hamhock asked.

"I think," I said, "we look for a bigger apartment."

Do other dads not end their phone calls with existential despair? Because that's what my dad does. Papa ends most of his calls with me the way you might close a conversation with someone you want to menace. "Anyway," he'll say, "I'll be here. Staring into the abyss." Or, when I have given him good news, "The talented will rule and the rest will perish in the sea of mediocrity." Or, when I have given him bad news, "I am sorry for everything that happens to you, as everything is my fault." He never ends with anything that couldn't one day be construed as a tragic and yet comic last word. He never just says goodbye because goodbye has no weight. Goodbye would not haunt his children if he actually did hang up the phone and then die of that heart attack he's been anticipating for the last quarter-century. Goodbye wouldn't be significant.

Papa and I are at our best when we're on the phone, every evening, fifteen- or twenty-minute chats that weave together and make me feel as though we are forever in contact. Usually Papa is witty and ironic and magnanimous with anecdotes about the past or advice for the future. When he started watching *The Wire* he answered the phone with "What up?" or "Who dat?" or some other linguistic appropriation that does not actually appear in the show. If I don't acknowledge this greeting (perhaps with a similarly enthusiastic, "It's ya boy"), he will say it another two or three times. It's important that you notice this good mood he is in, because it is fleeting.

After I brought Hamhock home, little about my and Papa's calls changed. We continued to not talk about him as we had during the lead-up to the trip. We talked about my work or his crushing ennui or about how the biggest tree in the backyard rotted and he had to get it taken out or how Raisin started to yell "HOW RUDE" anytime someone did something she didn't care for. We walked around the edges of my relationship, a boundary I was fine with because the alternative was not speaking. While Mom, slowly, began asking more questions about Hamhock, called him on his birthday, spoke to him after his uncle died to give her condolences, Papa resumed life as if nothing had happened. I liked it this way; I didn't have to acknowledge with my father the uncomfortable fact that I was an adult, and he didn't have to pretend he was happy about any of it. We just hit the buzzer and started all over again.

Some months after Hamhock and I decided to move in together, we miraculously found an affordable two-bedroom apartment in a quiet, leafy neighbourhood a few blocks away from his old place. I mentioned it to Mom and she acknowledged the information the way a computer might recognize a USB key: a fact she noticed without emotion. I slipped it into conversation with Papa and

he said even less, seemingly trying to reject the information the same way he conveniently "forgot" where my
brother lived before he got married to his wife. (Guess
what! It was with her!)

I prepared for the move without discussing it with my
parents, packing up the first apartment I had where I
paid rent without help from Papa, who used to slide me
a few hundred dollars every few months just to "grease
the wheels" even when I didn't need it. Hamhock and I
fought three times in two different Ikeas about couch
colours and the wood finishes of our new bed frame.
("I don't want it to look like a girl's apartment," he said
to me, so I forced him to hang a four-foot-tall drawing
of a lingerie-clad Sophia Loren in our kitchen, saying,
"Everything you see I owe to spaghetti.") On the morning
of our move, Baby Braga and some of Hamhock's friends
came over to lift my heaviest boxes, the ones filled with
books, with binders filled with notes, diaries filled out at
fifteen and transported across the country for some
reason. I didn't bother to call my parents. They didn't
want the details and I didn't want a fight.

Once we arrived at our new place, it came to our
attention that our landlord had neglected to finish
renovating half of the apartment. The stairs leading to
our basement were gone, just splintering planks of wood
in their place, the hardwood flooring in the bedroom
was unfinished, moulding was missing from the hallway,
and light fixtures hadn't been installed. The only rooms

that were habitable were the guest bedroom downstairs and the kitchen; everything else was awash in boxes and new Ikea furniture that we couldn't even put together because we didn't have the room. I wanted to call Papa and tell him about the indignity of moving into a half-finished space where we could only set up a bed downstairs and wait for our landlord to get to work. But I knew that instead of solemnly laughing together at this minor misfortune, it might just bump up the inevitable yet undesirable fight.

And so I went through the transition of moving in with a partner for the first time largely alone. For the first four months, we fought near constantly: he hated dishes, any dishes, in the sink, I wanted to burn all his shoes when he left them splayed out near the front door for me to trip over, he collected old copies of *The New Yorker* as though they weren't an obvious and tempting fire hazard, he wanted to drown my cat, Sylvia Plath The Cat, who tore holes in the new couch and then woke him up at five every morning with a little "Whrrrrrr?" I dug into Hamhock to look for fights. I wanted him to defend himself and get angry and a little mean because fighting is the only way I've learned how to be in love. I'd accidentally drop receipts next to the garbage instead of in it and wonder if it was worth it to just leave them there, see how bad I could make this, see if I could ruin everything from the inside out. Maybe if this relationship was weak, weak enough so I wouldn't have to make the eventual, impossible choice between my father and my boyfriend, then the universe could just do it for me. We would break and we could move on. Like most things, it just needed some pressure.

Being with Hamhock has never felt like a sacrifice, like an unnecessary burden. For my parents, though, it might have been. It changed things, as I knew it would. It was worth it to validate him, to make him real, to stop stuffing a T-shirt into his mouth every time my parents called so they wouldn't know a man was near me. But even then, the loss was clear. In the pursuit of honesty, of a greater intimacy with both my partner and my parents, I had to destroy it to rebuild. This was the work I had avoided for so long, the hard question no one stuck between two worlds wants to answer: *do I protect him, them, or myself from the truth?*

For weeks, Hamhock and I slept on the lumpy guest bed in the basement, my beloved old bed, the one my dad had bought for me when I first moved to Toronto. We wrapped ourselves in our blankets and held each other, as if we were on a raft swimming among our suit-cases filled with clothes and trinkets, boxes filled with books that, eventually, we'd have to negotiate space for, Sylvia Plath ducking in and out of crevices I couldn't reach. We struggled for sleep because our home was still just a place with all our junk in it, and we still felt lost. Hamhock and I were at our closest, and yet, everything felt distant and unattainable and painful. I wanted to call

Papa to ask him if he knew this feeling, but I already knew the answer.

The great irony of growing up is that it's often once you leave your parents' home that you understand them the most. You get less angry; they get less anxious. I think fathers, in particular, are supposed to soften in certain ways, to appeal to you more, especially when you're a woman. You're supposed to find even footing, with the fighting of your childhood finished with. If you're lucky enough to have non-abusive, non-dead parents in your twenties, it's nice to have them in your life as allies rather than wardens.

But my dad sometimes gives me the silent treatment when he's upset, or sometimes he explodes with joy, or sometimes he is so sullen with the inevitability of death he hardly wants to breathe. The silent treatments are, without question, the worst of his reactions: they can last a few days or a few months, can break without my even knowing it, can extend into my face-to-face visits, can poison the rest of the family if he wants. When I bought a laptop case he deemed too expensive ($32.99) in 2010, he didn't speak to me for ten days. When I decided to stay in Toronto for the summer of 2012 to intern instead of returning home after I finished university, he didn't speak to me for two weeks. In 2008, my mother went to the mall during his midday meal hour and he attempted to make a

tuna melt, burning his hand in the process. He spoke to no
one for forty-five minutes until he realized he was still
very hungry. (He wanted her to throw out the toaster oven,
too.) And a year and four months after Hamhock and I
moved in together, he shut down yet again, this time a
delayed response. Papa's sun is the brightest, so when he
decides to set, it makes for some very long, cold winters.

When we moved in together, I knew Papa would get
mad eventually, but it seemed like such a risk to not do
it for that reason alone. Papa gets mad about *everything*.
The older he gets, the more furious he becomes over
small indignities, little imagined insults. Once, while in
the car together, he half stated, half muttered, apropos of
nothing, "You live, you create things, you become a footnote in history. That's what happens when you get old.
It's a trage – IT'S A TRAGEDY."

None of this – the impatience, the frustration, the willingness to hold a grudge against an inanimate object – is new to
me. He's always been waiting for something to ruin his life.
When I was little and would pretend to be a doctor and he
my patient, he'd ask me surprisingly real questions about his
hypertension and cholesterol, when all I wanted to do was
"test his reflexes" by hitting him in the shin with a plastic
mallet. He colours with Raisin but wants her to do something more "cerebral" with her talents. "No, don't colour
like that," he says. "Colour in the lines. The lines! Well, if
you're going to do it that way, at least do some Cubist-
inspired art. Show your inner angst. Show how angry you

are at the establishment!" She frowns at him and tries to ignore his commands. "Yes," he says. "Colour Dora's face."

The only confusing part in his silent treatment over Hamhock is that it came more than a year after we moved in together, long after I thought we were out of any danger zone. Mom has, since, softened remarkably, promising to come visit, inviting Hamhock over when he's in Calgary for business. It took Papa, however, a year to connect with his anger, to ice me out, to deliver retribution in the worst way possible. Some days I can tolerate his moodiness. Others, I am so furious with him I want to throw the silent treatment back at him, as if I can out-rage the man I learned fury from in the first place. Then, other days, I want to shake him and beg for forgiveness. I'll say I'm sorry, even if I'm not.

It's been months since I visited home last, even longer since Papa first decided he was in touch with his anger. He didn't talk to me at all for an isolating eleven weeks and three days, passing me over to Mom for daily updates and ignoring my emails or attempts to pull humour out of him. Maybe he expected I would bend first, but when I didn't, he eventually crept his way back to the phone, speaking to me nightly like we once did, but now with less ease. He'll chat for two minutes or, if I am lucky, a full ten minutes, asking for updates about work and nothing else. But the undercurrent of any conversation with him is deep sadness, his disapproval over something that felt right to me but insulting to him. This is the newest version of him that I have, one that might finally be willing to talk but is always, somewhere, despairing. He'll try to crack a joke, but I know I'm the cause for this latest reticence. His rage was always predictably untenable so it's never clear what version of him I might get when I call. Sometimes he answers the phone wanting to discuss the minor ways he's been slighted, like how he thinks the Bluetooth in his car is racist for not understanding his accent or how my mother is trying to kill him and "she's not being subtle about it, either." Other times he answers just to fight, to tell me he's "disappointed," to prattle off non-sense about immigrant parenting that he believes only when he is angry about his wishes being ignored, and how I have irrevocably changed our relationship. Worse is when he doesn't answer the phone at all, letting Mom handle me, Mom who is now extra chipper, extra sweet, constantly cooing at me and telling me she loves me. She's making up for lost time, or rather, lost conversation. I notice when Papa wants his absence to be noted. Every cell I have recognizes how ineffective his moodiness is in getting me to change, how it hurts with no other real influence. I tried and I tried and I tried to break my relationship with Hamhock, to get him away from me, but it didn't work. So instead, I have to wait for what feels even less likely: that Papa changes, that he shifts, that he lets yet another thing go.

This loneliness is the worst case scenario I've always dreaded, the one everyone – even my own family – told me was unlikely, if not impossible. Rebellion isn't my strong suit, neither is love, and now I have to perform both. I miss Papa aggressively because this still feels so unfair, but above all, I miss him because I understand him and he makes sense to me. I get angry at toaster ovens (TERRIBLE FOR POP TARTS), and irate when people don't follow my advice. I'm not so good with the silent treatment but not for a lack for trying. I worry like he does, too – planning funerals and preemptively complaining about who might slight me or my family when I'm long dead. I miss Papa from before he knew the truth about me (even if I was desperate to just tell him the truth) because Papa was my blueprint for the rest of my life. It was a flawed life. I didn't always like the outlook. But it was mine.

In any case, Papa has never been the strongest person in the family – that's always been Mom, who carries everyone's burdens on her back. He's never been the most stubborn either – that's always been me. He's not even the most sullen – that's my brother, at least since my birth. But Papa will crack, putting his surly contemplations about my relationship aside for good and not just in temporary bursts, as suggested last week when he answered the phone with, "The vagaries of time are taking their toll" (believe that this is him in a good mood), or the month before when he ended our call with, "You are brave, you are too brave." Or at least I need to believe in his ability to let things go when they are ultimately out of his control, because otherwise we're both just alone, spinning separately when we're supposed to be in this together. I can wait for the inevitable, because it *is* inevitable: he will call me instead of waiting for me to call him, maybe opening with something simple and weird and delightful, and I will again forget that he has the capacity for such darkness. In its place, we can remember that we are inextricably sewn together the way children are with their parents, no matter his mood or my rebellion, and life will creep forward the way it always has: "No one should get married. And if you do get married, you should never have children. They drain you of your creativity and render you into a caricature of a shell. Know where we are? The mall, where else. Your mother is looking at garlands. What are they called? *Necklaces.* God, she always wants something else, doesn't she? Anyway. What are you up to?"

ACKNOWLEDGEMENTS

Books only exist because of their editors, so: thank you to
Kiara Kent, Martha Kanya-Forstner, and Anna deVries,
for their brilliant edits and for understanding whatever
I was putting down. Thank you, in particular, to my dear
friend Kiara, one of the best editors in the game, who is
always filling a wine glass to its brim and pushing it forward, saying, "Okay, what's the problem?" I'm sorry I
emailed you at 4 a.m. all the time.

Thank you to my agent Ron Eckel, who knew this
book before I did, and to whom I owe an incredible lot.
Thank to you to Kristin Cochrane and Amy Black at
Doubleday Canada.

Thank you to my friends at *Hazlitt*: Haley Cullingham, an ingenious editor who brought forth so many of the ideas in this book. Thank you to Jordan "GABBO" Ginsberg, my favourite co-worker, the best Work Dad, a generous editor and friend who has always been so patient with me. Thank you to Robert Wheaton, who gave me my first real job.

Thank you to my *BuzzFeed* colleagues, and my incredible editor Karolina Waclawiak, to whom I owe at least 30 per cent of this book.

Thank you to so many who listened to me whine about this project: Danny Viola, Adrian Cheung, Rudy Lee, Miranda Newman, Naomi Skwarna, Bri Tulk, Adam Owen, Danielle O'Hanley, Kellie Cornforth, Molly Coldwell, Anne T. Donahue, Andy and Tessa and Sam and Sara. I'm sorry! It's over!

Thank you to Matthew "Baby Braga" Braga. You are my best friend and a vessel of unceasing support. Everyone else is garbage.

Thank you to Barbora Simkova, my sister. Thank you to Sarah Weinman, my Book Mom.

Thank you to Scott Deveau, the love of my life who so often carries me on his back when I am too tired. Thank you for struggling for comfort with me.

Thank you to my family: my brother and sister-in-law, Angela and Jason and Connor, Neeta and Pankaj, thank you to Virangna and Bua and Fufa-Ji and Chacha and Chachi. Thank you to my grandparents who I never got to know, and to my aunties whose names I've never fully learned.

Thank you, always, to my parents, my complicated, nuanced, exhausting and yet calming parents. Mom, my favourite person, who so often has run her fingers along my scalp and said, "Everything turns out okay," and has always been right. Papa, our great protector, who fights and fusses with me in my every waking second but still calls to ask, "What is a schlemiel and how is it different from a schlemazel?" Thank you both for throwing me into the world and for pulling me back again.

And finally, thank you to Raisin, a ray of sunshine in this dark, ominous world. One day, all of this will make sense to you, or none of it will. I'm not sure what's worse.

Scaachi <sk@gmail.com>, November 24, 2016

my publisher wants you to write my author bio for the back of the book

Papa <papa@gmail.com>, November 24, 2016

Who would have the editorial control over what I write. I need some iron clad guarantee that they do not turn what I write which would be insightful and very succinct into some post pubescent pablum.

Scaachi <sk@gmail.com>, November 24, 2016

I have spoken to my editor and she has guaranteed that she will not edit you

Papa <papa@gmail.com>, November 24, 2016

You must correct it for punctuation which is elites trying to keep bourgeoisie like us down. Here it goes:

The author of this book Scaachi Lalita Koul is my daughter, born when both Wife and I were at the cusp of entering middle age but we were deliriously happy to welcome her after a particularly painful pregnancy. I am positive, or I would like to believe that she got a lot of her material from my musings which I expressed out loud to humour her. It could also be that I was vicariously living through her. I am almost certain she has presented me in a very poignant and loving way. Or again I could be delusional. If I am presented as crank or an Indian version of Archie Bunker then my revenge would be complete because I named her Scaachi with silent C.

A NOTE ABOUT THE TYPE

One Day We'll All Be Dead is set in Neue Swift, an enhanced version (2009) of Dutch type designer Gerard Unger's original Swift, created in 1985. It is an assertive type, highly readable in a variety of sizes and weights, with robust serifs, large counters and generous x-heights.